Hollywood is the place of dreams—people dream of being famous stars, writers, and directors. One in a million actually breaks through in the industry and makes it. David A.R. White is one in a million. But because he's done it without abandoning his Christian faith, which is part of his life since his Kansas childhood, he's one in 10 million! His remarkable story of dreams coming true without surrender to the secular is now captured in his fascinating book, *Between Heaven & Hollywood*. Funny, earthy, and real—it's as good as his movies!

GOVERNOR MIKE HUCKABEE, FORMER GOVERNOR
OF ARKANSAS, *NY TIMES* BESTSELLING AUTHOR

As a child I could daydream with great ease, and so many of the things I dreamed were realized with equal ease. But then as a child my trust in God also came so easily . . . then, I had a childlike faith. As time went on, as it undoubtedly will . . . the challenges of life . . . the many stumbling blocks and heartbreaks called into question that faith, demanding all the while that I deepen my relationship with God and strengthen my dependence on Him, if once again, the dreams He placed in my heart were ever again to become a reality.

I only wish I had this "gem of a book" to encourage me along my journey and make the path a bit more clear, as I surrendered the dreams in my heart to His purpose for my life. But I have it now. This book not only reawakens our ability to dream, it can reintroduce us to the greatest relationship of our lives. Dreams are but a vision of His Plan for Our Lives.

ACTRESS AND AUTHOR ROBIN GIVENS

Reading David's story, I felt at times I was reading about myself because our stories are similar in many ways. Citizens of Heaven, working in Hollywood. As he points out so eloquently, each of us is a deliberate creation of God, with a God-breathed dream inside us. And each unique, with a wonderful future—if we let Him lead us. I wish every young dreamer would read David's story; it's entertaining, sometimes funny, often inspirational, and eventually thrilling. And it's chock full of God's Word and will for all of us, but employed in individual and surprising ways. You've done big things, David—but this book may well be your best production.

PAT BOONE, ENTERTAINER

I met David when we worked together on the set of the Pure Flix film *Redeemed*. This book and how David lives his life are an inspiration to me and many others who feel called to work in the entertainment industry.

MEGAN ALEXANDER, NATIONAL TV REPORTER;
AUTHOR OF *FAITH IN THE SPOTLIGHT*

David's story will inspire you to honor God by pursuing the dreams He places in your heart. *Between Heaven & Hollywood* gives you a roadmap of how to overcome the challenges you will face if you seek to be a witness for Christ in the public arena.

DR. RICE BROOCKS, AUTHOR OF
THE BOOK *GOD'S NOT DEAD*

David A.R. White, in his book *Between Heaven & Hollywood*, has touched the human heart as he strikes a familiar chord with all people who desire to see their dreams fulfilled in their lifetime. In his popular movies *God's Not Dead* and *God's Not Dead 2*, we see him stand firm and fearless in his faith; being bold in his presentation of God's infinite character to a world who blatantly denies His existence. As with his work on screen, this book will enthrall the reader to aspire to the heights he has reached. He is a man who has defied the odds and demonstrated his persistence in pursing his dreams according to God's divine purpose.

RAUL RIES, PASTOR OF CALVARY CHAPEL,
GOLDEN SPRINGS IN DIAMOND BAR, CALIFORNIA

David A.R. White is a preacher's kid from a small town next to nowhere, with God-given dreams that pushed him naively and courageously into the Hollywood abyss. I trust and I have enjoyed working for and with David and was surprised because I thought I knew much of his successful journey into "The Business." I was pleasantly surprised to read of his trials and tribulations as he has proven to be a significant Hollywood player while armed with his faith and trust in God.

Between Heaven & Hollywood is filled with inspiration from a man who grew up on a wheat farm in Kansas without a single connection in Hollywood . . . except perhaps his connection to God. After reading this book I'm reminded of how deep his faith is, and why he was making Christian movies long before it was considered "good business." He has accomplished a small miracle: honoring the Lord while making successful profitable films of faith in Hollywood. This book is an inspirational guide to following your God-given dreams and reminds us that it's our unexceptional ordinariness that make us so uniquely extraordinary. Take a chance and read this book . . . it could change the way you see yourself, your faith, and how you go about pursuing your life and dreams.

TED MCGINLEY, ACTOR AND
STAR OF *DO YOU BELIEVE?*

Between Heaven & Hollywood elucidates the hidden tension within each one of us between the ache to pursue a dream and fear that we will fail. David A.R. White courageously challenges us to dream bigger and trust God more boldly. White masterfully draws us into his very personal struggle of dreaming big, relying on God more severely, and wrestling with fear of failure. *Between Heaven & Hollywood* inspires us to leave trepidation in the dust and hand our biggest passions to God.

MEG MEEKER, MD, BESTSELLING AUTHOR
OF *STRONG FATHERS, STRONG DAUGHTERS*

BETWEEN
HEAVEN &
HOLLYWOOD

CHASING YOUR GOD-GIVEN DREAM

DAVID A.R. WHITE

ZONDERVAN

Between Heaven and Hollywood
Copyright © 2016 by David A.R. White

Requests for information should be addressed to:
Zondervan, *3900 Sparks Dr. SE, Grand Rapids, Michigan 49546*

ISBN 978-0-310-34594-7 (softcover)

ISBN 978-0-310-34980-8 (audio)

ISBN 978-0-310-34595-4 (ebook)

David A.R. White is represented by The Litton Group, a brand management and content strategy agency in Brentwood, Tennessee. Learn more at www .TheLittonGroup.com.

Cover design: James W. Hall IV
Cover photos: Westend61 / GettyImages / © oneinpunch / iStock® / Cultura RM / Alamy Stock Photo
Author cover photo: Cathryn Farnsworth Photography
Interior design: Denise Froehlich

First printing August 2016 / Printed in the United States of America

To my parents,
Gene and Marcy White—

You taught me at an early age to love the Lord and keep him first and foremost in all my endeavors. For that, I am truly grateful. I love you, Mom and Dad, and I can't wait to see you again in heaven.

Contents

Introduction: Save Your Receipt 11

1. A Dream Is Born 15
2. Turn Right at Second Thoughts and Go Straight
   to the Other Side of Fear 35
3. I Have a Feeling We're Not in Kansas Anymore 55
4. God Wants You to Succeed—Sometimes 75
5. The Hard Part 93
6. Time to Stop Talking and Start Listening 111
7. When Plan "A" Doesn't Work, Remember God
   Has Twenty-Five More Letters 133
8. Don't Hate the Wait 147
9. If It Means Something to You, Give It Away 165
10. Now Get to Work 179

Epilogue 189
Acknowledgments 191

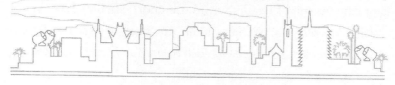

Save Your Receipt

*There's a time for daring and there's
a time for caution, and a wise man
understands which is called for.*

Dead Poets Society

I f you're reading these words, then you're probably standing in a bookstore with my book in your hands, trying to decide if this is the one for you or if you should perhaps get the one written by the guy with bigger hair. Or maybe you're browsing Amazon and taking advantage of the "Look Inside" feature before you decide whether you want to buy this book.

Good for you. I think we all would be better served if we gave a little more thought to our decisions before we invested our money, our time, our effort, or our love.

If, however, you have already purchased my book because of its catchy title or my award-winning smile or because you like my movies, then I want you to know how much I deeply appreciate your support and confidence in me.

Having said that, I hope you saved your receipt.

I have a nagging feeling some readers might not know what

to make of my book. I fear some will be suspicious of it, not so much because of its outrageous claims and grandiose promises, but rather because of the lack of them.

You are probably accustomed to seeing titles that guarantee fantastic overnight results with little effort, such as *Lose Weight While Overeating, Seven Steps to an Absolutely Perfect Life (Six, If Seven Is Too Many), How to Get Rich Before You Even Finish Reading This Book,* or *Learn Patience Instantly.*

If you have ever purchased these types of books, then I bet you wished you had saved your receipt. The truth is, many self-help books don't work. If you own more than one, there's your proof.

Listen, I make movies in Hollywood. I live in a city and work in an industry that specializes in hype, fantasy, and reality distortion. I know how to take a little bit of nothing and turn it into a whole lot of something. I could have done that here, in my first book. I could have exaggerated the claims. I could have made outrageous promises about how good this book would make you feel and how it would revolutionize your life so that you would consider yourself a fool not to buy it. I could have. But then after reading it you might have felt cheated or misled, and your dissatisfaction would pretty much guarantee there would not be a second book.

This book is about the realization of God-given dreams. It's about changing something intangible and ethereal into something tangible and concrete. It's about how you take what God has written on your heart and turn it into the writing on the wall. It's about living out a passion in the actual, day-to-day world.

In the upcoming pages I will demonstrate the principles of

dream realization by highlighting instances from my personal and professional life. As such, much of this book is autobiographical in nature, but it's not an autobiography in the truest sense. Each chapter opens with a story from my life, not to take a trip down memory lane, but primarily to illustrate and support the concepts and lessons I've learned along the way and intend to share with you. It's my hope that you will learn from both my victories and defeats and see real-world, practical applications of the ideas discussed.

I am not going to lie, mislead you, or sugarcoat the difficulty of this journey. Likewise, I will not misrepresent the biblical ideals I have included in these pages because:

1. They're not paying me enough and they never will.

2. I don't want to jeopardize my relationship with the Lord because (see 1).

3. I don't *have* to lie because the truth is greater and more satisfying than anything I could make up.

This book will not help you to lose weight, but it might encourage you to lose the fear and doubts that weigh you down. This book will not make you rich, but rather convince you to live richly. I cannot guarantee you a perfect life, but I can show you how to perfect the life you live.

Lastly, I ask you to do two things that may seem contradictory during your pursuit of dream fulfillment. I ask that you have faith in God, but also that you exercise caution and good judgment during your journey. Trust in the Lord, but leave yourself an extra twenty minutes on the highway in case of periods of heavy congestion. Know that God will ease your burden, but only pack what you can carry yourself. Pray for God's wisdom, but do your own research on a candidate before casting your vote. Fear not, for the Lord is always with you, but when it comes to important purchases, save your receipt. Matthew 10:16–17 tells us, "I am sending you out like sheep among wolves. Therefore be as shrewd as snakes and as innocent as doves. Be on your guard. . . ." For while the Lord God will never disappoint, rush hour traffic, luggage handlers, politicians, and retailers just might.

I'm done with the disclaimers. I hope I've clued you in to what this book is about and, just as importantly, what it is not. Are you still reading? Good. Then let's get started.

CHAPTER 1

A Dream Is Born

Somewhere, over the rainbow, way up high.
There's a land that I heard of once in a lullaby.

The Wizard of Oz

I spent much of my growing-up years in Meade, Kansas, a small town just outside Dodge City. That being said, have you ever heard the expression "Get out of Dodge"? It means to leave a troublesome or perilous environment as quickly as possible, as in, "I had to get the heck out of Dodge." The saying refers to Dodge City, Kansas, a bustling cattle town in the late nineteenth century popular for its corruption and the well-deserved title of "The Wickedest City in America."

Dodge City is the site of a famous series of gun battles called the Dodge City War and hosted such colorful characters as Wyatt Earp and Bat Masterson. Its checkered past made it a favorite setting for movie and television Westerns in the early to mid-twentieth century.

By the time I got there, however, the cowboys, saloons, and gamblers had long since moved west, and Dodge City had become a sleepy, quiet little town much like others in western

Kansas. The city traded in its brothels and bars for meatpacking plants and wheat and sorghum farming. I'm not sure what sorghum is, but I am familiar with wheat—more on that later.

My years in Kansas were spent in a small Mennonite Brethren community. As I write this, I'm looking outside my window at the palm trees swaying in the gentle breeze of the Los Angeles landscape, and I am reminded there is a time difference between the West Coast and my quaint little Mennonite town in Kansas. For instance, right now in California it's 12:55 p.m. and back there it's 1956. And just so you know, I'm not necessarily convinced that is a bad thing. Mostly.

Perhaps you aren't quite sure what a Mennonite Brethren is. Mennonite Brethren are Christians; that is to say, they believe in the lordship and saving grace of Jesus Christ and in the triune God—the Father, Son, and Holy Spirit. Although they share ties to other types of Christianity, the Mennonite Brethren are neither Catholic nor Protestant and—most importantly—they are not Amish. Although the Mennonites and Amish originate from similar traditions begun in the sixteenth century, there are significant differences in how the two groups live out their Christian values. For instance, the Amish generally shun modern technology, refrain from political and secular involvements, and wear odd-looking hats.

Mennonite Brethren, on the other hand, are permitted to use electricity, such as the type used to power electric razors, and therefore have no good reason to walk around with those goofy-looking beards. While the Mennonite Brethren are not nearly as hard core or conservative as the Amish, they do make the Mormons look like a pack of Hell's Angels.

I grew up a churchgoing kid. Then again, I didn't have much

of a choice because my father was a preacher in the Mennonite Brethren Church, and every Sunday he brought us to work with him.

SON OF A PREACHER MAN

As a preacher's kid, I was aware of the spiritual realm much earlier than a lot of people. For instance, I accepted the Lord into my life at the ripe old age of four. Which is strange, when you consider no court of law anywhere in the world would consider a contract signed by a four-year-old legally binding. By the time I realized what I had done and what I had pledged to forgo until my wedding day, it was too late.

Much has been written about the lives of PKs, and I see no reason to add to or revisit any of it here. I'm sure you've already heard how our families typically have to move every four years or so to the next church and how we have to share our parents' time and resources with an entire congregation. You've probably heard we're held to a different standard in terms of our good behavior and spiritual maturity. In pop culture, PKs are categorized as either repressed, wound-tight Goody Two-shoes who end up in a bell tower with a high-powered rifle or we're angry, heroin-addicted atheists who wear too much Goth-inspired mascara. I have never been either of those. I'm proud to have had parents who sacrificed and devoted all they were and all they had to the service of God. There are times, however, when that service can be overpowering for a child. While I learned at a young age that being part of a ministry family could occasionally be difficult, I never felt the need to wear mascara. Just saying.

My parents instilled in me a strong work ethic from a very

early age by assigning me chores, duties, and other responsibilities. I appreciate having that quality now, but at the time I lacked the foresight to understand the value of a hard day's work. The whole ordeal was annoying because it got in the way of doing the things I enjoyed, like catching frogs or building tree houses.

PICKING ROCKS

I remember the first job I ever had, and looking back I can't decide if my parents had my best interests in mind or simply didn't like me very much. I was about nine years old and in the fourth grade when I was hired to pick rocks out of farm fields. I was a rock picker. Rock Picker is not a glamorous title nor is it a particularly exciting job, but there you have it. Unless you grew up on a farm, you might not understand the importance of rock picking. Allow me to explain.

In addition to whatever crop the farmer happens to be cultivating, some fields tend to also grow rocks. They propagate in a variety of sizes; some start out no bigger than your fist, but if you're not diligent in removing the rocks they can quickly grow into boulders. The pesky and invasive rocks that grow in a farmer's field not only have the potential of damaging expensive farm equipment, but they also take up valuable real estate that could have been seeded. Seeds will not grow on top of or underneath rocks, so they must be picked up, and that's where I came in.

Rock picking usually involves taking a wagon or trailer pulled by a tractor out to the field, walking up and down looking for rocks, and then picking them up and throwing them onto the trailer. In my case, the rocks were then transported to someone else's field, where presumably another nine-year-old fourth grader was hired to pick those rocks out of that field and bring them back to ours. The cycle is infinitely self-perpetuating, which explains why rocking picking is a time-honored and ancient profession. I think that's how it went. At least that's the way it seemed to my nine-year-old self, who would rather have been anywhere doing anything else.

I don't want to leave you with the impression that I was lazy or that I shied away from hard work. Nothing could be further from the truth. For one, I was making four dollars an hour picking rocks, which allowed me to buy *Star Wars* action figures when they came out. Even at nine years of age I had my priorities straight.

Nevertheless, despite my tender age, I wondered if there were something more enjoyable I could do that would still allow me to buy my toys. Something that was more fun but also paid me lots of cash. I believe the expression is *having your cake and eating it too*.

After a few years of rock picking and other mind-numbing jobs I was forced to do, I began to acknowledge that, for me, certain work was pure drudgery. At the same time I also accepted much of this work was unavoidable and often necessary. I began to realize that if I had to work, then I needed to learn how to work smarter. It took me a few more years, but I eventually figured out that some kinds of work were just more appealing to me than others, and if possible I would trade up from the work I didn't care for to the work I preferred.

In an attempt to save money at the grocery store, my parents kept and maintained a huge vegetable garden. Actually, they kept it, but their children maintained it. The first of their free laborers were my older brother and sister, but as soon as I came of age, the task of weeding this massive expanse fell on my shoulders.

I'm not talking about a cute little plot of ground where my folks grew the occasional tomato plant or begonia. I had to weed an enormous tract of land with dozens of types of fruits and vegetables. If memory serves, there were far more weeds growing than rutabagas and cauliflower, so much so that oftentimes I couldn't tell the difference between them. By the way, I have since learned that vegetables are much easier to pull out of the ground than weeds. I learned this lesson the hard way.

Ralph Waldo Emerson once wrote of weeds, "What is a weed? A plant whose virtues have never been discovered." No disrespect intended to this great American poet, but I am here to tell you Ralph never weeded my parents' garden. If he had, he might have changed his mind about the virtues of weeds.

I grew to detest weeds only a bit less than having to go out and pull them. I accepted that this had to be done, and I knew why my budget-conscious parents were growing a garden in the first place, but in order to save my back and knees, I needed to think of a better way. I needed to work smarter and come up with a compromise.

That's why in my freshmen year of high school, I purchased a riding lawn mower. You're probably thinking it was my intention to ride over the weeds, mowing them down and then calling it a day. My parents would not have gone for that, so I had something far more creative in mind.

I planned to use the riding lawn mower to start my own lawn-mowing business so I could pay my parents not to grow a garden. I asked them to calculate how much money they saved at the grocery store each month by growing their own produce, and then I told them I would pay them that amount each month instead of tending a garden for our family. It was my idea for how to eliminate a job I disliked and offer a compromise I hoped my parents could not refuse. They were speechless when I first presented my plan to them, but after some consideration they found no other option but to agree with my logic.

At fourteen years of age, I started David's Lawn-Mowing Service. I drove that riding mower all over town, mowing people's yards wherever and whenever I could. I made decent money that summer of my freshman year in high school, even after subsidizing my parents' nonexistent vegetable garden.

At the end of each month I wrote my parents a check from the money I made, and thereby eliminated the need for a garden and freed myself from the bondage of having to weed it.

I can't swear to it, but I might have even seen a glint of admiration in my father's eye when he would show neighbors the exact location of the garden where he wasn't growing corn. "And over there is where we're not growing potatoes. Next year," he would muse, "I'm considering not growing strawberries."

I don't consider what I did to have been lazy. I think of it as knowing myself, understanding my limitations, and working within the boundaries and confines of the system. At the time, the "system" was comprised solely of my mom and dad. It wasn't so much that I wanted to "beat the system," but rather to *navigate within it* and arrive at a mutually satisfactory destination. I learned the invaluable concept of compromise from negotiating with my parents. Of course I could not have known it then, but this was a skill I would employ time and time again much later in my professional life.

A couple of years later I heard the US government had devised a similar arrangement with our nation's farmers where under some circumstances the government would pay the farmers not to grow certain crops. Now you know where they got the idea! And you thought this book was going to be a lot of self-aggrandizing fluff.

During the summer of my sophomore year I was talked into working with my brother, who had a small business painting houses. I have very little to say about my summer of house painting other than it wasn't for me. Since I couldn't pay people not to paint their houses, I elected to exercise the next best option. I quit.

AMBER WAVES OF GRAIN

The summer of my junior year my dad thought it would be a wonderful and life-enriching experience for me to "go on harvest" and work on a wheat farm. I learned that two important inventions were responsible for the sudden surge and popularity of wheat farming in 1930s America.

The first was the development of the combine, a machine that aids in the harvesting of grain crops by combining three separate functions into one piece of equipment. The combine made harvesting wheat easier and less expensive and therefore more profitable.

The second invention largely responsible for the popularity of wheat came out about the same time as the combine. Toast.

Yes, you read that right: toast. Around this time the automatic bread slicer had been perfected, and a couple of years later the automatic, spring-loaded toaster was introduced into homes. America would never again eat breakfast the same.

You may wonder why I am telling you all of this. You might even be thinking, *I'm not reading this book to hear about combines and toast! What's this guy going on about?* I point these things out because they are what I had to tell myself that summer while driving a combine or tractor across a wheat field when there were plenty of other "teenaged guy" things I would have rather been doing. It's always hot when you harvest wheat; either that or it's raining. "So how did you spend your summer vacation, David?" Wheat, heat, and rain.

By the way, I am allergic to wheat. Don't get me wrong, I'm not talking about a "Quick! Throw him down and stab him in the heart with an epinephrine auto-injector!" type allergy. It's more the sneezing, coughing, and runny nose kind of allergy that leaves you so miserable you wish someone would throw you down and stab you in the heart with an epinephrine auto-injector. I am sure there is a marked and valid difference between the two, but at the time I had considerable difficulty discerning what that might be.

I learned something about myself from my experiences picking rocks, pulling weeds, painting houses, and harvesting wheat: although these were noble pursuits in their own right, none of them were for me. It wasn't that I thought I was better than these jobs or that they were beneath me in some way. I didn't realize it at the time, but the problem was that these jobs didn't match the dream I had for my life. For as long as I can remember, the only thing I wanted to do was to go into the entertainment industry. This dream consumed my daily thoughts. I was interested in the cowboys and desperados of Dodge City, mostly because I wanted to be one. I enjoyed playing with my *Star Wars* action figures because I imagined myself as Han Solo or Luke Skywalker, traveling across the universe righting wrongs with my lightsaber and blaster. I knew I could never actually be a cowboy or Han, but I wanted to be the guy who got to portray him on the big screen. The frustration and boredom I felt while riding a combine began to crystalize this vision. All along, my discontent was trying to tell me something, but it wasn't till I was eighteen, during my last summer on the farm, that I began to realize it.

LISTENING TO THE WHISPERS OF MY DREAMS

It is when you are stuck doing something in your life that you would rather not be doing that you often find yourself thinking most about what you would rather be doing. Your uncomfortable reality and your lofty dreams make for strange yet compatible bedfellows. One can't exist without the other. One gives birth to and continually nurtures the other.

To put it simply, if you feel the life you are living is empty, vacant, or unfulfilling, then it's possible your dreams are trying to show you a better way. Dreams are like exit signs prompting you to get off the road to nowhere. Which is why we must listen to the whisper of our dreams, for they are the doorways to happiness and a satisfying life. Your dreams are your ticket out.

It was during this process of bemoaning one life and coveting another that I started paying attention to my inner voice, my calling. By the way, it's referred to as "a calling" because if you're not listening then you might not hear what God is trying to say to you. During my last summer on the farm, I began to listen.

I had no choice because there was little else to hear. Have you ever heard the sound wheat makes when it's growing? The silence is deafening. If you ever need to be alone with your thoughts, I mean *really alone*, then go sit in the middle of a wheat field. The boredom left my brain on pause and my heart open, both begging for meaningful discourse. I'd be out in the fields with nothing but wheat in front of me and wheat behind me, and I suspected there was something different for me out there. Not out in the wheat of course, but way, way out there beyond the wheat. About 1,200 miles past the wheat to be exact, in a mythological city called Hollywood. Truth has a way of sneaking in when you're alone with yourself, partly because despite the way it may feel, you are never truly alone. God is always there, and sometimes he uses these quiet moments to communicate with you. For lack of anything else to distract me, the quiet of the wheat field made it easier for me to hear his whisper. His whisper came in the form of a desire—a dream, really.

I couldn't understand it. Why acting? Where did this desire come from? The whole thing was a bit ridiculous. My exposure to acting and the dramatic arts was extremely limited. We did own a television, but it was rarely on because the Mennonite Brethren frowned upon television as too worldly. It wasn't until I was eight years old that I saw my first movie in a theater, and believe me when I say that the adventure came about completely unintentionally. I was out with my friend and his parents, and they took me with them to see the movie *Grease* with John Travolta and Olivia Newton-John. It was a magical experience. The sound and images on screen were incredible. Even though I was sitting with an entire audience, it was as if I were taking my own trip into an incredible fantasy world. My enjoyment was tarnished only by the fact that, after seeing Ms. Newton-John in her skintight, black leather pants, I was convinced my soul was now consigned to eternal damnation. It would be another ten years or so before I ventured back into a movie theater.

The acting bug bit me in seventh grade when the high school English teacher, Mrs. Rooney, cast me in the role of Kurt in the high school production of *The Sound of Music*. I was more than flattered. I was validated because Mrs. Rooney typically cast only experienced upperclassmen and yet she chose me, a novice and a middle schooler no less, to play what I considered the most important role in the musical. I remember thinking Mrs. Rooney must have seen through all of my shortcomings and recognized my raw yet undeniable talent. Looking back, I think it was probably less about my talent and more due to how short I was and that I looked more like a young kid than any of the juniors and seniors, who were already six-foot plus and sporting whiskers.

While putting on the clothes and makeup was a little weird, I loved the theater. In a way it was like being in a time machine; for an hour and a half I was catapulted into another life, another world. I've always been a huge fan of people's stories. I find them fascinating; I think if I hadn't gone into the entertainment industry, I might have gone into journalism. The other thing about the theater was, when the lights go down, there's electricity in the air. Anything can happen—it's like the actors are on a tightrope. That's why live theater will never be replaced; it's similar to a sporting event, except you're able to transport yourself into the story. There's something so exciting about it all. And to me at that time, I was hooked. I felt alive.

By the time I got to high school, the theater program was involved only in producing musicals, and since I don't have the greatest singing voice, I pretty much sat out. Other than a bit part as a munchkin in *The Wizard of Oz*, my experience on stage was limited; our school had no drama classes or acting lessons. Most of my classmates were interested in farming or sports, so even though I had begun to realize that what I really wanted to do with my life was to act, I knew very little about how to go about it. I was too embarrassed to share my dream with anyone or even talk about it, because I was clueless about the acting field in general. I had no idea how or where to start, what it would look like when I got there, or what obstacles might be in my way, but as I sat in that wheat field, I knew acting was a dream I had to pursue.

WHAT I DIDN'T KNOW DIDN'T HURT ME

If I had known then what I know now about the entertainment industry, I might not have chased my dream. I'm sure the impossibility of it all would have overwhelmed me, and I would have talked myself out of it. Believe me, most people would have advised me to let go of this dream, telling me it was a childhood fantasy. Because of my insulated upbringing, I possessed a wide-eyed innocence, making me the last person on earth who should have left all that he knew, moved to Hollywood, and entered into arguably the most cutthroat, competitive, "only one in a million survive" industry on the planet.

However, in retrospect I can see my naïveté served me well. I was too dumb to know what I didn't know, and my ignorance gave me confidence. Not an ideal situation, but I'll take it. Bottom line, I wasn't afraid—and that is a good thing when it comes to pursuing your God-given dream. If you allow fear to get in your way, to stop you from getting to where God wants you to be, you run the risk of a far less rewarding and fulfilling life than what could have been.

My dream of a successful career in the entertainment industry was my beginning, my starting place. The finish line was still far away, so far away I couldn't even see it clearly, which is surprising when you consider how flat Kansas is!

What is your beginning? Where is your wheat field, and what waits for you beyond it? These are not rhetorical questions. You are going to need to answer them and be very clear about your answers if you ever hope to live your dreams. In order for you to fulfill your dream, you must first identify it. This is critical, but I don't believe it is the first step. I believe your journey begins by understanding where that dream came from in the first place.

THE ONLY "YOU" GOD EVER MADE

During the "in the beginning" days of the universe, when God first created humankind, I imagine he used a specific and unique genetic blueprint for each and every one of us. There is and never will be anyone exactly like you. Psalm 139:14 reads, "I praise you because I am fearfully and wonderfully made; your works are wonderful, I know that full well." In the original Hebrew text, the word *wonderfully* means "unique, set apart, and therefore uniquely marvelous."

Do you have a hard time accepting this? Are you having difficulty imagining that of all the bajillion people on the planet Earth, God created no two exactly the same? It might be easier and more palatable for you to simply refer to God's unique blueprint for you as DNA. That's fine. Call it what you like, but I would like to point out that the Swiss chemist Friedrich Miescher first identified DNA some three thousand years after David wrote about being "wonderfully made." Just saying.

I believe God included a dream, a destiny, and a uniquely specific reason for living in each of our unique blueprints (DNA).

We are told in Romans 12:6, "We have different gifts, according to the grace given to each of us."

Here's what I believe is a plausible backstory to this verse. I am oversimplifying this process, but I picture God pondering his creation and concluding that he needs something specific done here on Earth. Perhaps he knew a certain community would one day need a leader, or that it would need a bridge built at some point, or maybe even that a child somewhere would need to laugh at just the right moment to give him the strength to persevere in his battle against a life-threatening disease.

God saw what he wanted done here on Earth, so he said, "I'm going to need someone to do _____ for me. It has to be just the right person with all the right qualifications. I should probably then make this person." So he took a little bit of this and a touch of that and he created *you* to do this specific thing. He conceived and designed you to do it better than anyone else. There is a certain way your heart loves that nobody else can duplicate; a unique way you process information that nobody else can imitate; a way you relate to people; a particular sense of humor you have; a unique way of singing, telling stories, building a business, designing, or decorating. You bring something to this world that no one else can deliver. You please God unlike any other. Your dream is inside your heart, but it didn't start there. God put it there, and now it lives within you.

I suspect that some of you reading this are doing a quick inventory of your talents and your special attributes and somehow coming up with nothing. You have concluded there is nothing special or unique about yourself, and therefore God has nothing in mind for you to do for him. You feel as though God has left you to fend for yourself.

You might have come to this erroneous but nonetheless dangerous conclusion for many reasons, but one comes to mind that I see a lot in the entertainment business. My guess is, you are comparing yourself to people our society celebrates, and as a result you feel less than special.

We live in a culture that glorifies certain talents and attributes while ignoring others. Much is made of the NBA player who repeatedly and without fail sinks the ball from the three-point line or the young woman whose voice wows the celebrity judges on *American Idol*. These people are elevated to the status of superstars and royalty and are rewarded with vast sums of money and adoration. "He has a God-given talent," they say, or "Her voice is a gift from God." It appears logical to us that people who are so blessed by the Lord would be successful in their chosen endeavors.

What about the talents and gifts that are not so obvious or the dreams that don't seem so grand? What of the basketball coach with the gift of organizing and fund-raising who imagined building a community gymnasium and, after ten years of work, finally realized that dream, offering a place where young athletes can begin to realize their own dreams? What of the piano teacher who led a children's choir and in doing so introduced music into the lives of children and instilled in some of them a great passion for singing?

Unsung heroes? Maybe, but I tell you this. When people achieve their God-given dreams, heaven sings for them. What else really matters?

Every day I meet people who feel they are nothing special. It reminds me of a disease, actually. It's almost like some kind of illness that has spread like a virus throughout our society, causing people to look into the mirror and see so much less than what God sees when he looks at us. God sees more because he can see into our spirits. He is not distracted or dismayed by the external, what exists only on the surface. First Samuel 16:7 tells us, "The LORD does not look at the things people look at. People look at the outward appearance, but the LORD looks at the heart."

There are tons of suggestions and explanations as to why there might exist a type of institutionalized epidemic of low self-esteem. I have heard it theorized that advertisers need for us all to think less of ourselves so we'll buy their products that promise a new and improved life. Some say it's a result of social media; others suggest uninvolved caregivers or early emotional trauma.

Whatever the road or reason that leads people to despise or think less of themselves, their assessment of themselves is erroneous. It is a lie that they are less valuable or significant than anyone else. I know this to be true, for there are piles of Scriptures announcing God's love for each individual soul. Here are just a few:

> Humble yourselves, therefore, under God's mighty hand, that he may lift you up in due time. Cast all your anxiety on him because he cares for you. (1 Peter 5:6–7)

> See what great love the Father has lavished on us, that we should be called children of God! And that is what we are! The reason the world does not know us is that it did not know him. (1 John 3:1)

> But because of his great love for us, God, who is rich in mercy, made us alive with Christ even when we were dead in transgressions—it is by grace you have been saved. (Ephesians 2:4–5)

The LORD your God is with you, the Mighty Warrior who saves. He will take great delight in you; in his love he will no longer rebuke you, but will rejoice over you with singing. (Zephaniah 3:17)

We are, after all, each and every one of us, made in his image. Do you think that when it came to you, God made a mistake? Do you imagine that in the very instant you were created, God was distracted and you were shortchanged?

You might be thinking I am giving you too much credit. *David wouldn't say this about me if he really knew me. I'm far from special. I'm not particularly educated. I'm not successful. I have no illusions of grandeur.* You might also be thinking, *Actually, if you get right down to it, I'm a seriously flawed individual. I don't live a perfectly righteous life—far from it. I'm not the kind of person God would have a special plan for.*

If you remember nothing else in this book, remember at least this: It doesn't matter where you were born or what kind of life you had growing up. Maybe as an adult you have felt unappreciated or even rejected. Maybe you've had your share of bad luck and misfortune or suffered great tragedy. It is not an accident or random chance that you are here on this planet. You are here for a reason—and that reason, that unique destiny, is found in your God-given dream.

There is no one too common, too ignorant, too uneducated, too poor, too inexperienced, or too broken and sinful that he or she cannot be used by God to achieve his goals.

You think I am the one giving you too much credit? Actually, I'm not the one giving you credit—God is! At the end of the day, what difference does it make what I think? Or what your boss, teacher, spouse, neighbor, or anyone else thinks? God has faith in you. He thinks you can do what he created you to do.

"In the beginning" refers not only to the creation of time, space, and matter. It also refers to the conception of you and me and the dreams God has instilled in each one of us, dreams to do specific tasks that he needs done on this planet.

Now that we've established that your dreams are not entirely your own, that they exist because God gave them to you and that God thinks you are worthy of these same dreams, you may be thinking the hardest part is behind you. If so then you should probably turn to chapter 2.

For photos of David's childhood, his early jobs, and his first acting role, go to DavidARWhite.com/Exclusive.

Turn Right at Second Thoughts and Go Straight to the Other Side of Fear

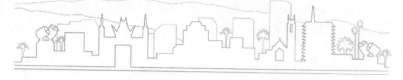

*Don't let fear cheat you out of your dreams. God
is bigger than whatever you're worried about.*

Unknown

In eighth grade, I watched a movie that would change my life forever—*Rocky III*—and I watched it repeatedly. I knew every line and could do bad impressions of every character in the movie. "I'm afraid. For the first time in my life, I'm afraid!" Seriously though, that movie packed in so many life lessons, including: Never give up, and whatever you do, don't go into a fight right after your manager just died. Sylvester Stallone wrote, directed, and starred in this enormously successful film, and he became my hero.

So inspired was I by Stallone's achievements in *Rocky III* that I would often catch myself fantasizing that he would one day get lost while traveling through Kansas, pull over, and ask me for directions, and as a result my life would be forever changed.

"Hey, uh—excuse me," Sly would mumble in the way only he can. "But, uh, I don't know where I am. All these roads, you know, they look the same. Maybe you could help me get back to Hollywood?"

I would shield my eyes against the harsh midwestern sun and answer politely, "Yes, sir, Mr. Stallone, sir. You just have to get back on the highway and continue west on Route 54."

"Hey, thanks a lot, kid. You know, come to think of it, I could use a bright, polite guy like you to costar with me in my next movie. As long as it's okay with your parents, y'know what I mean?"

This fantasy was as far as it went when it came to my planning and preparing for a career in show business. I know. Ridiculous, right?

HIDDEN SECRETS

I spoke very little to anyone about my dream of working in the entertainment field. It was just too different, too unorthodox for the folks in my community, and I feared I would no longer fit in if I spilled the beans. I was afraid they would think I was crazy for believing I could move to Hollywood and become a movie star. Perhaps deep down I was afraid they were right. The few times I mentioned it to my parents, their response was pragmatic. "Son," my father would begin, "you don't know how to sing or dance, so that's not an option."

I couldn't argue with him. My father was right. I was not blessed with a singing voice, and as a Mennonite Brethren I was forbidden to attend dances, so I never had a chance to pick up any dance moves or even find out if I had a natural talent. The thought of dancing or singing in front of people filled me with so much anxiety and apprehension that to this day I get uncomfortable even watching musical theater.

Mrs. Thomas, our school librarian, once asked what my plans were for after graduation. I think I mumbled that I wanted to move to Hollywood and become an actor. Her response was measured and matter-of-fact: "I think you'd make a great actor." I couldn't believe she said that. She was the first person who thought my dream wasn't stupid. I'll forever be grateful to her for validating my life choice. I held onto her encouraging words, despite the fact that I knew I would not be going to Hollywood after graduation. I never had any question, any doubt, as to where I was headed after high school.

THE RULE

My father had one rule that all of us kids had to abide by. It didn't involve picking rocks, weeding gardens, or working on a wheat farm; those things I learned to navigate around. My father firmly and without negotiation insisted that after high school graduation, his children must attend Moody Bible Institute in Chicago, Illinois, for at least one year.

Moody is a conservative Christian college specializing in careers for students interested in Christian ministry, counseling, and education. My father's dream for me was that I would follow in his footsteps and become an evangelist, and Moody was a step in his plan for how I would achieve that dream.

Not only had my brother and sister graduated from Moody, but both my father and mother had graduated from there as well. As a matter of fact, Moody was where my parents first met each other. Likewise, it was at Moody where my sister met her husband and my brother met his wife.

Are you sensing a pattern here? Not only was Moody Bible Institute a time-honored establishment of higher learning with a reputation for training generations of preachers and church leaders, it was also an opportunity for the Whites to widen the gene pool. There were only eighteen young women in my high school graduating class. There were thousands of available coeds at Moody. You do the math.

While my parents were calculating the statistical probabilities of my scoring a life mate at Moody, I was contemplating the realities of living in the Windy City. Even though I didn't want to go to Moody and didn't want a career in the ministry, I was oddly comforted knowing what the next year of my life entailed. My friends were stressing about their college choices and anxious over their futures, but mine was all planned out. I didn't have to figure out what I'd be doing for the next twelve months, nor was I burdened with accountability, because I had no say in the matter. My father's ultimatum stirred my sense of duty but also triggered in me a sense of relief—kind of. For the time being, I was content to stall my dream and put it in the "someday" category. After all, I was still young with plenty of "somedays" in my future, but right now I needed to buckle down, get a college degree, and be responsible.

THE WINDY CITY

So that is how it came to be, in the fall of 1988, that my parents and I set out in their Ford LTD for Moody Bible Institute.

Moody's campus is located in the Near North Side of Chicago and is 881 ground miles from Meade, Kansas, about a fourteen-hour drive. I spent the majority of that ride wondering how I was going to figure out the "acting thing" while at Moody.

Even though I had not abandoned my dream of succeeding in show business, I still had not told anyone of my secret intention to go to Hollywood. I told myself that Chicago just might be the gateway to my dream. After all, I had a much better chance of meeting Sylvester Stallone on the side of a road in Chicago than I ever did in Kansas.

I remember when I first drove into Chicago and how I felt when I saw those massive buildings looming high above me. On the one hand, I was ready to leave the nest and be on my own as a young man. On the other, I had a nagging fear that Chicago would swallow me up and spit me out. I had never experienced anything like the city before, and I was overwhelmed. The city was too bright, too noisy, and too expensive. There were too many streets with far too many addresses to remember. For me, Chicago was a vast and impersonal city too easy to get lost in and too easy to be ignored by. I wondered, *What am I doing here? How will I be able to drive my car through all of this traffic? What if I am recognized as a country rube and someone tries to sell me a bridge? How will I afford to live here? How can I stand out amongst so many different kinds of people and make my mark?*

Despite my conflicted feelings, when I said goodbye to Mom and Dad on the steps of my dorm room, it could have been a scene in a Norman Rockwell painting. I promised my mom I'd be home for Christmas and assured my dad there'd be no horseplay at school and that I would treat the whole college thing seriously. There may have even been mention of my yet unknown bride-to-be. Despite my apprehension, I assured myself all would be fine. After all, my parents believed I needed to be at Moody. What could possibly go wrong?

TIME TO GET TO WORK

As pastors of a small midwestern church, my parents couldn't afford to help me much financially during my tenure at Moody. Although tuition was free, I still had to pay for room and board, so getting a job was one of the first things on my agenda.

Luckily, a local valet company liked to hire Moody students to park cars for the city's restaurants and nightspots because we often turned out to be the most honest of the company's employees. I quickly found a job parking cars for some of Chicago's hottest attractions like America's Bar, Ditka's, and Harry Caray's.

In the 1980s, Chicago's sporting teams reigned supreme, and I was right there in the middle of it, parking cars for the city's most celebrated athletes. It was a nonstop party for the Bulls, Bears, and Cubs, and the air crackled with electricity, especially in downtown Chicago. Just imagine what it was like for a small-town kid from Kansas to be driving around in Walter Payton's Testarossa, Michael Jordan's Ferrari, or any one of Scottie Pippen's vast collection of expensive automobiles. I learned to drive a stick shift on a Porsche in the parking lot of the Steppenwolf Theatre, where I would later watch performance after performance of Gary Sinise and John Malkovich in Steinbeck's *Of Mice and Men*. It was the first professional play I ever saw. I was mesmerized at what they were able to do. I loved the fog, the sets, the crisp, cold air in the theater. I was alive, and I wanted to do what they did.

That year, I grew up in so many ways and had so many different experiences. For instance, I went to almost every Chicago Bears home game. People would leave at the end of the first or second quarter, and they were happy to give me their ticket stub. I'd stroll into Soldier Field like I'd been going to games my whole life. I was living the dream. I wasn't living *my* dream, of course, but at least I was having fun living my parents' dream for me. I kept busy and distracted. I barely noticed the time ticking by.

Looking back, I am struck by my level of naïveté during that first year at Moody. I lacked what many call "street smarts," as there weren't many paved roads in Meade, Kansas. One particular story comes to mind that illustrates my innocence and perhaps even ignorance as to my new surroundings.

One night while I was parking cars for Ditka's, the valet staff was given brand-new pairs of promotional Kangaroos sneakers, those trendy tennis shoes that came with a small zippered pocket on the side. At quitting time—three in the morning—I decided to save some time getting back to Moody by cutting through Chicago's infamous Cabrini-Green public housing project.

Yeah. So there I am with a couple hundred dollars in cash folded up in my pocket, twisting my way through dark alleys, past piles of garbage stacked many stories high right in the middle of gangland central, when I am stopped by three very large African-American men. "Where'd you get those shoes?" was all I heard over the pounding of my heart.

This is where I die, I thought, *all over a silly pair of sneakers with an even sillier pocket sewed into the side.*

It turned out the man asking me about my shoes was legendary Chicago Bears running back Walter Payton. Apparently he had just signed an endorsement deal with Kangaroos and was genuinely interested in my thoughts about the sneakers. So instead of dying that night, I spent fifteen minutes discussing the benefits of a shoe pocket with Walter Payton in an alleyway of Cabrini-Green at 3:00 in the morning.

I would like to tell you I learned a lesson from that evening, but I'm afraid that would not be the last time I tempted fate, acting impulsively or even foolishly with little regard to consequences. Clearly, I had the Lord's hand of protection around me, but in the months and years to come, I fear my rash spontaneity may have tired the Lord somewhat. I'll get to some of that later.

WHAT DIDN'T HAPPEN

I could tell you more stories about what happened to me during my freshman year at Moody, but I think it far more important to point out what didn't happen.

I did not learn much about acting. Only that I was driven to pursue it. Moody isn't what you would call "drama friendly." The only drama group offered at the time was one that focused on mime. (No, I'm not kidding. And yes, I did it, but I wasn't very good at it.) Bottom line, I did not have access to the proper resources while at Moody, and although I was disappointed, what could I do?

I did not meet my soul mate. While there were many interesting young women to meet, a whole cornucopia the likes of which I would never have met in Kansas, I kept to myself and did not have time to date.

I did not fall in love with the idea of becoming a missionary or an evangelical preacher. In fact, after only a few months at Moody, I became even more certain that ministry was not the path for me.

I did not return to see my parents at our home in Kansas over the Christmas break. As a matter of fact, I never went back to that house while my parents were living there, and it would be well over a year before I would see my parents again.

You may ask how I managed *not* to do so many of the things

I was supposed to during my year at Moody. The answer is both simple and complicated, but in the most straightforward terms I offer this: *I was not meant to.* I was not meant to live out anyone else's dream for my life. While I was distracted from pursuing my dream by pursuing my parents' dream for me, God was busy at work in the background, using circumstances and events to further his plan for me.

AN UNANTICIPATED TURN OF EVENTS

The year I was studying at Moody, parking cars, and trying to mime, my father called me and gave me some hard news.

"Son, your mother and I will not be living in Kansas any longer. We've put our resignation in and are looking for a new church."

I muttered, "Why, what happened?"

I couldn't believe it. My dad had done so much good in this town. He had pioneered the first Christian radio station in southwest Kansas in order to minister to the farmers who spent many hours on their tractors. In addition, he had started a prison ministry. I couldn't understand why my parents had to move away. I felt as if I'd been punched in the gut. We'd moved a lot when I was growing up, and I hated the thought of our family moving again.

I didn't know why or how, but I believed that my parents had been wronged, and that's why they were leaving. They were not the type of people to share too much. They always wanted to protect the church. They never wanted to show disrespect to God or others, and it was very important for both of them to live in purity and peace with all. It was years later when I found out that my father had been let go from his position as pastor, although "let go" is not an accurate term. After some damaging rumors were spread, the parishioners chose not to reelect him after his six-year term had expired. Suddenly and without warning, my parents found themselves without a job, with little money and no idea of what tomorrow would bring.

I have little more to say about this experience other than that it hurt my family and it hurt me. I wanted to fight back, to have justice. It wasn't fair.

Even so, my parents remained friends with those at the center of the rumors. In the years to follow, many of the parishioners who voted my father out later contacted my parents and our family to apologize for not standing up for the truth or defending what was right. Even though my father was wrongfully incriminated and all of our lives had been turned inside out, my parents and I forgave those involved. After all, we are Christians, and forgiveness comes with the territory.

I remember very well my shock, sadness, and frustration when my parents called from Kansas to tell me what had happened. However, a second bombshell was about to drop that in some ways overshadowed the first. My father accepted another job as a pastor in Saskatchewan, Canada, and my parents were planning to leave our Kansas home immediately. It was almost too much to absorb. Saskatchewan? They could have told me Mars and I would have been no less affected. My parents' decision to move to Canada was a pivotal moment in terms of the direction my life would take.

NOT AFRAID

After my parents delivered the news, I hung up the phone and experienced a clarity I had not yet known in my life. A career in ministry, although never my first love, seemed even less attractive now that I saw how my parents had little control of their destiny and were subject to the whims of their congregation. They made less than thirty-five thousand dollars a year and sacrificed so much in order to preach the gospel. A pastor is on call 24/7. There is always someone to visit in the hospital or hospice. There is always another wedding or funeral to attend. My father worked around the clock for little or no appreciation or recognition, and yet he and my mom never complained. They knew what they were getting involved in when they accepted the call to ministry, and they accepted it wholeheartedly. Ministry was my parents' calling—but I knew it wasn't mine.

I also came to the realization that many of the things I did and the decisions I had made since graduating high school were based on or influenced by fear. I was living someone else's dream for me because I was too afraid to take responsibility for my own life. I spoke little of my desire to be a Hollywood actor because I was afraid of people's negative reactions. I busied myself with routine and distractions in part because I was just a kid looking to have a good time, but also because I was afraid to take an honest inventory of my year at Moody. Keeping busy kept me from facing and dealing with my fears.

Fear and self-doubt allowed me to buy into the *someday myth*. Look at any calendar and you will notice that "someday" is not a day at all. Proverbs 27:1 assures us today is the only day guaranteed us when it says, "Do not boast about tomorrow, for you do not know what a day may bring." If pursuing our God-given dreams is what life is all about, then it follows that procrastination can be considered irresponsible.

Fear prompted me to lay blame on others or on less-than-ideal circumstances. While it is true that Moody lacked resources for those interested in the dramatic arts, I failed to exploit the resources I *did have* access to, like the many theaters, drama groups, improv troupes, and acting coaches all within three miles of Moody's campus. As long as I could blame something else for my inertia, I wouldn't have to own it and be responsible for it.

Ultimately I was afraid of failure, and at nineteen I was fully convinced all failure is bad—irrevocably and irreversibly bad.

After I hung up the telephone with my parents, I was surrounded by a silence and stillness that I had not experienced in several years. It was as if I were back in the wheat fields of Kansas, alone with the Lord. I could once again hear the whisper of my dream, and I realized my fear had created the biggest obstacle in the way of my dream. And that obstacle was me.

I called my folks after the Christmas break and told them I was going to finish out the year at Moody, but soon after I wanted to go to Los Angeles to become an actor. My parents had enough on their plates dealing with their sudden upheaval and relocation to Canada. After a brief silence my father said, "As long as you serve the Lord in whatever you do, we support you."

I hung up the telephone and never gave the matter a second thought. I was going to pursue my dream. I was going to become an actor. I was no longer afraid.

While it's encouraging to know God is the author of our dreams and that he wants us to succeed, we nevertheless must accept that many times and in many ways we get in the way of our own success. It seems counterintuitive because, if asked, everyone will say they want to accomplish their dreams and goals, and yet we allow obstacles and roadblocks to prohibit our dreams from coming to pass. The most villainous and destructive of these obstacles is *fear*. If you allow it, fear will—without mercy or hesitation—stop you from doing what God has called you to do.

You may have heard that the phrase "do not be afraid" or "fear not" is written in the Bible 365 times, and that those verses serve as a daily reminder from God to live each day fearlessly. You may also have heard that as sweet as that sentiment is, it's not accurate, and no translation of the Bible has that many mentions of the whole "fear not" thing.

I can assure you of two things: (1) I'm not going to go through the Bible and count how many verses tell us to "fear not," because (2) it doesn't matter to me. If the Bible tells us only once not to be afraid, then that's enough for me, and I hope it's enough for you too.

I suppose I could end this chapter here and simply say you shouldn't let fear stand in the way of achieving your dreams and goals because God said you shouldn't, but as a longtime member of the human species, I know it's not as simple as that. I'm not going to mince words; fear is an insidious monster. Fear of what could happen can ensure nothing will happen. But as with all monsters, fear can be defeated—especially when you realize it's a monster of your own design and it only has as much power as you give it.

Oftentimes fear is the thing that will keep you from taking the next step along your path of dream fulfillment. You're aware of where you want to go; you can even see it on the horizon or just around the corner; but when you visualize taking that next step, no matter how big or small, you find yourself paralyzed and unable to continue. To make matters worse, sometimes fear can cause you to retreat to that safer place of just wishing, sacrificing whatever progress you may have managed thus far. All of this approach-and-retreat, two steps forward and one back, amounts to a colossal waste of time, and if you're not careful, a waste of your life.

I did little while at Moody to advance myself closer to my dream because I focused solely on the issues of the day, like making pocket money and studying music. It's amazing how much time can fly by when you are not paying attention. You think you are getting things done, but then at the end of the day you wonder why you are not happy or why, despite all the checks on your to-do list, you feel unfulfilled. Keeping busy was in many ways a defense mechanism. As long as I was distracted from facing my fears, I didn't really have to deal with them. We can stay in this place for years because the "unsettled feeling" pales in comparison to the bone-crushing anxiety associated with fear. *I'm unhappy*, we think, *but at least I'm not terrified about what the next day will bring.*

We must learn to accept that oftentimes taking the next step to our dream is frightening. And that's as it should be. For many of us, it *needs* to be frightening because moving forward in the face of fear is how we grow as people and how we grow in our faith. God tells us, "Do not fear, for I am with you; do not be dismayed, for I am your God. I will strengthen you and help you; I will uphold you with my righteous right hand" (Isaiah 41:10). God tells us that the more fearful we are, the more we need to lean on him. In that way we discover his strength. Whatever lies ahead of us, no matter how daunting, is not as great as the power behind us.

WHAT FEAR DOES

If you have a God-given dream, it's going to be big, unreasonable, illogical, unwieldy, and seemingly impossible. No wonder you feel afraid! However, God is telling you right up front, "I've put this desire into your heart, and you're going to need me to get there." If left unchecked, fear can paralyze you and keep you from achieving the goals and dreams he has put into your heart.

In other words, fear can actually stand between you and the Lord. That unhappiness you feel when you're not pursuing your God-given dream, that sensation of discontent, is a message that you're not living the life God has intended for you. Worse, you have allowed fear to challenge your relationship with him.

I said fear was like a monster, but it's a monster of your own invention. Did you know we are only born with two fears: the fear of falling and of loud noises? All other fears are learned through our own or others' experiences.

Let that sink in a moment. Whatever your fears comprise, whether fear of acceptance or of failure, you are the author of those fears. Think of it as your version of Frankenstein, which you created in the basement of your mind. Just like the mad scientist in the old story, you have to face your monster head-on and take back the power you've invested into it, or you run the risk of it standing in the way of dream fulfillment. Many times we only react to fear instead of observing it. We flee from it instead of taking back control of it, and in doing so we continue to feed fear.

Fear wants your happiness, your hope, and your future. I have heard fear likened to a thief in the night, but fear is sneakier than that. The weird thing is, fear is less like an alleyway mugger in a rough part of town and more like a beggar. Fear will not demand you hand over to him all that is precious in your life. No, this guy is cleverer than that, more insidious.

Fear will get everything he wants from you because you will give it to him willingly.

How? Because fear knows you, he's well aware of what makes you tick, and he knows the buttons to press. He will lean in and whisper those things specifically designed and tailored with you in mind to trigger self-doubt and insecurity.

"You're not smart enough."

"No one likes you."

"You'll go broke chasing your dream."

"You're not attractive enough."

"Your chances of success are a million to one."

"You will fail because deep down, you know you're not good enough."

And fear will wait as long as it takes for him to get what he wants. Don't ever doubt fear's unrelenting patience with you. He's got all day. Fear has all the time in the world. Fear has the entirety of the rest of your life. He will stand between you and your dream until you hand your future over to him. He doesn't have to mug or rob you because you will give him all he desires. Willingly.

OVERCOMING FEAR

Scared yet? I hope you are. Here are some things I have learned along the way about how to deal with fear.

Use Your Fear

The first thing I'm going to encourage you to do is for you to partner with fear. That's right. I want you to use fear to make fear an unwilling ally in your journey to dream fulfillment. I hope when you face fear in whatever dark alley life has in store for you, you turn and run—right into the arms of God.

Turn to God

Yes, I said it. I want you to run right to Daddy. Run to your heavenly Father as fast as you can and ask for his courage. Turn your focus away from all of the obstacles you feel are in your way (real or imagined) and concentrate on God, who is capable of anything.

After I learned my parents were leaving Kansas for Canada, I got alone with God and asked for his comfort and guidance. I gave my fear over to him and asked that he replace it with courage and peace of mind. And he did!

This is something fear does not want you to do. God is to fear like kryptonite is to Superman. God is like the bucket of water to the Wicked Witch of the West from *The Wonderful Wizard of Oz*. In your darkest, most dreadful hour, keep your eyes fixed only on Jesus. "So we fix our eyes not on what is seen, but on what is unseen, since what is seen is temporary, but what is unseen is eternal" (2 Corinthians 4:18).

God is both the dream giver and dream maker, and he has already conquered every enemy that seeks to discourage you from fulfilling your dream and God's dream for you. In simplest terms, he's got it covered.

Take a Chance

Once you are imbued with the courage of the Lord, take a chance. Have faith that God is watching out for you, and go and do something that will get you closer to living your dream.

Whatever your dream is, it's going to require action in order for it to come true.

For me, taking a chance meant I had to stop wasting time, stalling, procrastinating, and letting others dream for me. I had to commit to a serious pursuit of my acting career. Although I didn't know exactly what that looked like at this stage in my life, I vowed to figure it out.

For others, taking a chance might mean quitting your day job, taking a class at a community college, investing time into your spouse, or sticking up for yourself and fighting for what you're worth. Maybe you need to mend the fence with an old friend or lend a hand to a person in need. Whatever it is, stop letting fear hold you back and start doing.

Don't get me wrong; a leap of faith doesn't mean you should go off foolhardily without a plan or preparation. I made this mistake when I decided to go to Hollywood, and I will talk about it in a later chapter, but for now, yes, please have a plan. But don't overplan. Overplanning is just a stall tactic conceived by fear. Have courage and make that leap. Psalm 37:24 tells us God will catch you. Do not let your fears choose your destiny. Instead let God choose it for you.

Surrender

If you're starting to feel anxious and breaking out into a cold sweat thinking about actually chasing your dream—good. You should feel totally vulnerable and exposed, because it will make you aware of your complete dependence on God. Only by surrendering your life to him will you get to live the life you were meant to live. His way.

Don't spend too much time thinking about a "Plan B" or a way out if you fail. I believe a backup plan is an insult to the Lord. I've heard it said that if you have something to fall back on, then you probably will at the first sign of difficulty. Have a little more faith. If down the road God leads you to a different path than the one you started on, then by all means change tracks. God has millions of second chances ready for you at a moment's notice, but let him make that call for you. Let God plan an alternative route if he feels it necessary. Trust him completely and *go for it!* Don't let your fear of what could happen allow nothing to happen.

I used to tell myself, "Take delight in the LORD, and he will give you the desires of your heart" (Psalm 37:4). Remember we're talking about *your* heart. Not your parent's, not your spouse's, not the author's of the last self-help book you read—*your heart.* Be careful not to live someone else's plan. Don't be afraid to take responsibility for your own life.

Courage is not the absence of fear but the triumph over it and the understanding that what lies on the other side of fear is something worth risking everything for. And courage is something we need when taking a chance to pursue our dreams, because, as we'll see in the next chapter, the road to dream fulfillment can be rocky, and at times it can really stink.

For photos of David during his days at Moody Bible Institute, visit DavidARWhite.com/Exclusive.

CHAPTER 3

I Have a Feeling We're Not in Kansas Anymore

Most of the time God's promises are in your reach—they are not in your hand. You have to go and get them.

Pastor Tony Evans

S omewhere about thirty minutes into a movie, the main character will make a decision to commit to achieving a goal. The character may decide to challenge the heavyweight boxing champion of the world, plan to rob a Las Vegas casino, or simply gather up the courage to date the person of their dreams. After this grand and dramatic declaration, the filmmaker may show us what is called a montage.

In filmmaking, a montage is an editing technique where several different shots from different locations are joined together in order to compress time and deliver a lot of information. Typically music will play over the montage, adding to the excitement as the character prepares to embark on an adventure. One of the best examples is the training montage from the movie *Rocky*, the one that ends with the title character running triumphantly up the steps to the Philadelphia Museum of Modern Art.

If someone were to make a movie of my life, it would include a "Gonna Fly Now" montage right after the scene when I told my parents I was moving to Los Angeles to study acting after finishing the year at Moody. The series of shots might have taken place over my last few months in Chicago and could have included packing up my possessions, poring over Los Angeles newspapers looking for a place to live and a place to work, calling ahead to enroll in acting classes, writing to Los Angeles–based actors in search of advice, and finally driving cross-country aided by an AAA TripTik. The montage would end with swelling, victorious music, my beat-up car parked directly under the world-famous Hollywood sign, a symbol that after months of hard work and preparation, I had finally arrived in the land of my dreams.

The implication would be that from that point on, I would be living my dream. But that isn't what actually happened, because while I had a dream, I did not have a well-thought-out plan for how to achieve that dream. What actually happened is that I didn't have a clue about where to start, what to do, where to go, or whom to talk to when it came to pursuing my dream in Hollywood. I had a dream but no real goals. So when my year at Moody ended, I was a ball of zealous enthusiasm, but I had no idea where to take it or what to do with it.

Goals are like baby steps one must take in order to achieve the greater dream. I had a big-picture view, but I lacked knowledge of the smaller steps I needed to take to get from Moody to where I wanted to ultimately be. For lack of a plan, I did what many people do in a similar situation: I jumped on the first thing that was directly in front of me, because at least it felt like forward movement.

WHERE MY "WING AND A PRAYER" MENTALITY LED ME

The thing I jumped on was an ad in the student newspaper for an intern to work on a Christian film to be shot in Chicago. It sounded like a job for me. The film was to be produced and directed by Edward McDougal, who was already being called the Roger Corman of Christian movies. I first met with him at a hospital where the ever-frugal McDougal was able to buy me lunch in the cafeteria for only three dollars. The film was called *Across the Line,* and although McDougal didn't cast me in the movie, he did hire me to work as a production assistant. There was very little money involved, so I moved into Mr. McDougal's house for half the summer.

As soon as *Across the Line* wrapped, McDougal's production company immediately went into production of another film called *Geronimo* that was shot at a camp in Madison, Wisconsin. I spent the second half of that summer living in a cabin babysitting inner-city teens experiencing their first trip to the country. Although I was given a line in the movie, I was mostly working crew again. Once again I was doing a job that wasn't for me. I felt like I was wasting my time sitting in a cabin when I should have been in Los Angeles pursuing my dream. It wouldn't be until many years later that I would realize the value of this period of my life and how God can use any situation, no matter how mundane or boring you may think it is, for his good. Still, I really wanted to get to California.

I appreciated the opportunity of working with Edward McDougal, but as the summer ended, I knew it was time to move on. I had managed to save about $1,500 that summer, so I bought a ticket to San Diego, where my sister, Michelle, and her husband, Abel, were living. San Diego isn't Los Angeles, but at least it's in the state of California and wasn't a cabin in Wisconsin. Of course, if I had done a little research and some planning, I would have realized that $1,500 wasn't nearly enough for such a big move, but I was still operating on a wing and a prayer. Somehow I was okay with leaving the details to the Lord. After all, I told myself, God wants me to be happy. My mantra had always been, "Take delight in the Lord, and he will give you the desires of your heart" (Psalm 37:4). I'll let God sweat the small stuff.

I figured I could stay with my sister and my brother-in-law and use their house as a base until I got a job and found a place of my own. What could possibly go wrong?

Michelle and Abel were newly married, and she was pregnant with their first child. I knew from the moment I stepped into their very small home that my time there was going to be much shorter than I expected. It's not that they wanted me to leave; it was just bad timing, as Michelle was nesting in preparation for her newborn, and I was a disruption they did not need. I was just in the way.

Additionally, I was shocked to discover how expensive rent was in Southern California. My savings would barely cover the security deposit. I had no idea what I was going to do. I wasn't prepared for all that was waiting for me in San Diego. I wasn't in California for seven days before I faced the possibility of being homeless. Again, for lack of planning, my dream almost ended before it began.

Oddly, it was Abel's parents, Louis and Amparro, who came to my rescue. They offered me a room for rent in their three-bedroom home. About a week after moving in with Michelle and

Abel, I left their house and moved in with my brother-in-law's parents. Admittedly not an ideal situation, but I had painted myself into a corner and was left with few alternatives.

One of the first things I did after I settled in with Louis and Amparro—and when I say "settled," I mean unpacked my one suitcase—was to enroll in Southwestern College just south of San Diego in Chula Vista. My parents had instilled in me the necessity of graduating from college to the point where I felt as though if I didn't, I would be a failure no matter what else I accomplished in life. (Not incidentally, it took me about fifteen years to finally be okay with not graduating from college.) I still did not want to disappoint my folks.

My present course of action was clear: get a job, enroll in college, and try to build my acting résumé. I felt good that I had started to make goals for myself, but without any real idea of how to achieve them, they were mere wishes (more on that later). I needed to purchase a reliable form of transportation in order to do those things, so . . .

I bought a motorcycle. You may be tempted to flip back through the pages of this book to find where I mentioned I was proficient in riding a motorcycle or where I dreamed of owning one. Don't bother. You won't find it because I wasn't and I didn't. I bought a secondhand little Honda because it was all I could afford. In my well-laid-out plans for coming to California, I neglected to budget for a car, so this was going to have to do. I'm not saying the bike had Hello Kitty decals on it, but it might as well have.

For the next six months I tooled around San Diego on my little motorcycle, working the graveyard shift at UPS, going to college from 8 a.m. till 3 p.m., and then, after a few hours of sleep, heading off to play rehearsal. Oh, I didn't mention play rehearsal? In an effort to bolster my acting résumé I landed a part in the chorus of the rock opera *Macbeth*. You know, on account of what a great singer and dancer I am. It was my job to die a few minutes after I appeared on stage. The rest of the time, I was relegated to the back of the stage, where I pretended to sing with the other members of the chorus who were also killed moments after their characters appeared on stage. Don't judge me. It was a stage, it was California, and I was desperate.

After six months in San Diego, I spent an afternoon trying to get some much-needed sleep before I changed from my UPS uniform into my tights for *Macbeth*. I remember lying there wondering if I had made a terrible mistake. Not about the tights per se. I'm talking about the whole thing: the move to San Diego, the college courses, and the job at UPS. While I was doing something and paying the bills, none of these things were getting me any closer to my dream. I was running in place, keeping busy, but not getting anywhere. I had enough of that at Moody. And the tights—definitely the tights. Performing in the chorus of *Macbeth,* I felt like I was back in the wheat field. The only difference was this time I was much closer to the Land of Opportunity. You could practically smell the smog of LA from where I was living. Something had to change.

It was in late February and cold by Southern California standards when I saw an ad for an acting class on the FOX Television lot in Los Angeles. I decided that if I was ever going to get anywhere in this business, I was going to have to start making some more productive moves, so I enrolled in the class. Los Angeles is about a 120-mile drive from San Diego on Interstate 405. At nineteen years old, I'm thinking, *It's a two-and-a-half-hour drive, at night, on the freeway, during the winter, on a tiny motorcycle and back again. Yeah. I got this.* Obviously, I didn't think it through. Do you see a pattern emerging here?

By the time I arrived on the FOX TV lot, I was frozen solid from both the wind and fear. I looked like a mixture of Jim Carrey and Jeff Daniels in *Dumb and Dumber,* in that scene where they dismount from their minibike after a crazy cross-country journey to Colorado. I hobbled into the acting class and took a seat in the back, hoping no one would notice me while I thawed out. A few minutes later I excused myself to go to the restroom and wash the dead bugs off my face. What happened in there would be my first real breakthrough toward fulfilling my dream. Seriously.

I was washing my hands at the sink when I met Brian Brody, a positive and charismatic motivational speaker who had worked with Tony Robbins. He mentioned he had noticed my state of disarray when I entered the class and wondered if I had been mugged or something. I contemplated telling him I had been in order to save face, but I instead confessed that it was just a long drive on a "Hello Kitty" motor scooter all the way from San Diego. After he finished laughing, Brian did a very strange thing.

He told me that if I ever decided to make the big move to Los Angeles, I could stay with him in his apartment on Venice Beach. He then gave me his telephone number, probably expecting to never hear from me again.

I had the long drive back to San Diego at 11:30 p.m. on my souped-up moped to think about Brian's offer, and by the time I got home my mind was made up. I called Brian the next day and our conversation went something like this:

"Hello. This is Brian."

"Yeah, hi, Brian. It's me. David White."

"David . . . ?"

"We met in the bathroom last night."

"The bathroom . . . ?"

"Yeah, you said if I ever decided to come to LA, that I could stay with you."

"Oh, yeah. You're the kid from Kansas with the Minnie Mouse motorbike. So you're thinking about making the big move, huh?"

"Yeah. Would tomorrow be okay?"

"Um . . . okay, I guess."

And so a few days later I rode back to Los Angeles on my motorcycle so that I could move in with Brian. A friend followed behind me with my bed in his pickup truck and to watch out for me in case a stiff breeze blew my scooter off the highway. All the way there I envisioned how cool it was going to be living with Brian in his bachelor pad on Venice Beach. Finally, my dreams were coming true. *Los Angeles, here I come!*

"HELLO, REALITY. MY NAME IS DAVID"

Brian was happy to see me when I arrived at his place, and he promptly showed me the kitchen—where I would be sleeping. Thinking back on it, the odd thing was, it was more weird for me than it was for him. Now, in all fairness to Brian, he may have mentioned that he lived in a studio apartment when we first met back in the restroom on the FOX lot, and maybe he had been looking for a roommate to live in the kitchen, but it's also clear I didn't understand what that meant. Once I set my bed up, his refrigerator doubled as my headboard. If I ever woke up in the middle of the night wanting a glass of water, I could conveniently turn the faucet with my foot.

As it turned out, the real-world demands of living in Los Angeles were much the same as the demands of living anywhere else. I needed a job, and Brian helped me find one at the Los Angeles International Airport driving a baggage cart for US Air. I enrolled at Pierce College and signed up for a full course load, including an acting class, and tried my hardest to figure out how to get an agent so I could land some acting work and build my rather thin résumé. That didn't work out the way I had hoped either.

I didn't realize how hard it was to get an agent. Apparently I wasn't the only person in Hollywood looking for representation. Who knew? Actually, I'll tell you who knew: those who did their research and groundwork before moving to Hollywood, that's who. If I would have given this some thought while I was still at Moody, I could have written some letters or made some overtures from there. Instead I just showed up on agents' doorsteps asking if there was anyone willing to help me. Not smart. Just another example of my "wing and a prayer" mentality and how I lacked direction.

Oddly, my first audition in Hollywood didn't come by way of an agent, but rather through my friend Jeff, the very same friend who hauled my bed in his truck from San Diego. Jeff was a dancer and told me about an open call for Madonna's Blond Ambition World Tour. He asked me if I wanted to tag along. Well, who wouldn't want to meet Madonna? He told me it was unlikely she would actually be there, but still, I was curious about the audition process and looked forward to an opportunity to get out of my kitchen-bedroom so I could uncross my legs.

So there I was, trying to be invisible and looking like a farmer in my flannel shirt and boots amidst hundreds of professional dancers. They were all wearing fancy dance gear and doing their stretches when an audition coordinator for the tour asked me if I was there to audition as well. I shrugged my shoulders and said, "Sure. Why not?"

I don't know why I said that. I've told this story a hundred times and each time I am asked that question, I have never come up with the answer. It just came out of my mouth. When I gave him my name—David White—the audition coordinator chuckled, "You sure are." Until that moment I hadn't noticed I was the only Caucasian there in a sea of dancers representing the entire racial spectrum.

Imagine my surprise when only ten of us were ushered into a small room and shown a series of complicated dance moves by none other than Madonna and her two backup dancers. Not only at this point was I an untrained dancer, I had never danced a step in my life (unless you call dying in the musical version of *Macbeth* dancing!). Now I found myself with The Material Girl as she demonstrated "The Robot" and "The Roger Rabbit." There was nowhere to hide, no one to stand behind. It felt like it was just Madonna and me. She asked, "Ya got it?" and before I could manage a reply, the music kicked on and I was tripping over my boots, my arms flailing like a broken windmill.

About sixty of the most humiliating seconds of my life later, Madonna turned off the music and mused aloud, "Hmm . . . who should we keep?" Everybody laughed when one of her dancers said, "How about the white guy?" They shared a smile. As I walked out, my face burning red with embarrassment, Madonna smiled and said, "Thanks for making my day."

COMFORTABLE IN THE UNCOMFORTABLE

The next four months were not much better. Because I lacked a plan, I also lacked a mentor, someone who could have guided me in the decisions I was making and helped me stay on track toward my goal. Consequently, I went from job to job. The gig at US Air didn't work out because I needed to be available during the day for auditions. I worked in a banquet hall for a while, but I had a problem understanding my immediate supervisor because I didn't know a word of Spanish and my supervisor wasn't fluent in English. I kept reminding myself that this was part of *paying my dues,* I was meant to be here, and soon things would turn around for me.

I did finally land a job in the movie industry working as an extra in the film *The Doors*, starring Val Kilmer and Meg Ryan. I was in the crowd during a couple of concert scenes. It was so strange, because almost everybody in those crowd scenes thought they were really at a Doors concert and were actually smoking marijuana and doing drugs. It was surreal and a bit creepy. I remember hoping that not all movie sets were like this. I didn't move to Hollywood to stand on a sound stage and get high from second-hand pot smoke.

Don't get me wrong—even at nineteen I understood the concept of starting at the bottom and paying my dues. But I quickly began to see how desperation and disappointment mixed with loneliness and displacement are a dangerous recipe for the human spirit. I began to understand why so many who had come to Hollywood before me, chasing the dream that had been part of their soul for as long as they could remember, ultimately referred to the town as the Land of Broken Dreams. I could see why so many had left with broken hearts and, more often than not, just plain broke.

Eventually I landed a job at Enterprise Rent-A-Car with flexible hours that allowed me to go out on whatever auditions I was able to muster without an agent. I was able to be comfortable in the uncomfortable, but not too complacent, something you never want to be. I remained hungry and kept my ear to the ground so I wouldn't miss an opportunity.

One day while at Enterprise, I heard about a casting call for high-school-aged extras to play on a football team for a new television show called *Evening Shade.* I was almost two years out of high school at this point, but I figured if I could dance for Madonna, I could play football for a high school. Besides, the show was to star Burt Reynolds, and I figured maybe I'd get a chance to meet The Bandit himself. That had to be worth something. Right?

If you take anything away from my story in this chapter, I hope it is the importance of having a plan, of setting some goals for how you can bring your dream to reality.

In order to write effective goals, you need to understand the difference between wishes, dreams, and goals. This is critical.

THE DIFFERENCE BETWEEN WISHES, DREAMS, AND GOALS

Oftentimes you will hear people use the terms *wishes, dreams,* and *goals* interchangeably, as if they were the same thing. I'm sure you've been asked, "So what are your goals in life?" or "What is your dream?" Even though wishes, dreams, and goals are interconnected, there are profound and clear differences between them—and understanding those differences can keep you from wasting time and effort pursuing your dreams in the wrong way.

A *wish* can be comprised of just about anything your imagination can muster. A wish is not obliged to follow any logical thread, nor does it instigate any action on the wisher's part. It's just something your brain does for fun on its down time while your body is busy with the mundane or riding atop a combine through a wheat field.

You've had wishes before. You know what they are. For example, you may have wished:

1. To unearth a pirate's treasure in your backyard.
2. For a flying horse.
3. That Sylvester Stallone would get lost in your hometown, ask for directions, and then bring you back to Hollywood with him.

I feel safe in assuming, however, that none of the above is on your bucket list. You don't plan to excavate your backyard. You're not eagerly anticipating that scientists will genetically engineer a winged horse, and you're not hanging around the highway waiting for Sly to drive by. At least I hope you're not.

Unlike wishes, dreams are passions you can achieve and should commit to. They are more than fantastic notions providing amusement and entertainment or relief from boredom. Your dreams are the keys to your future. Your dreams define who you are, and setting and achieving realistic and well-thought-out goals will help you accomplish your dreams.

The difference between dreams and goals is subtle, but it's

important we make a distinction. A goal is simply a well-defined and specific target. While it's true that a dream is also a target, it's the big-picture, broad-side-of-a-barn kind of target. Goals are smaller targets that act as stepping-stones to get to the bigger target that is your dream.

Dreams are your journey's final destination. Goals are the directions, strategies, and transitional steps you will take in order to see your dream to fruition. Dreams represent what you want and why, while goals represent your plan to get you there. Dreams can be big and seem unrealistic at first glance, whereas goals are focused and specific and therefore oftentimes more easily managed. Some dreams could look five to ten years into your future; others could even span your entire lifetime. Goals are short-term and rooted in the here and now, the foreseeable future. Sensible goals lead to the best results, or as Proverbs 21:5 tells us, "The plans of the diligent lead to profit."

Now that you understand the difference between wishes, dreams, and goals, let's talk about how to write an effective goal.

SMART GOALS

While researching this book, I came across something called SMART goals. SMART is an acronym used to describe well-defined goal statements. It stands for Specific, Measurable, Acceptable, Realistic, and Timely, and I think this formula deserves a closer look and perhaps a little biblical polish.

Specific

How many times have you heard someone say, "My goal in life is to be happy" or "I want to get in shape"? In Hollywood I often hear from those who have just arrived, "I want to become rich and famous." People often express goals that are too vague or too broad in scope.

Ask yourself, What is it that will make me happy? What does being in shape look like to me? What would have to happen in order for me to consider myself rich? Famous? Unless you are specific in what you want, it's hard to know where to start, let alone how to keep going.

It's best to narrow your scope when articulating your goals. For instance, instead of saying your goal is to be successful, you might say, "I have a goal to be promoted at my job within the next six months." Instead of saying your goal is to be physically fit, you might say, "I'm going to join a gym with the goal of working out three times a week for at least one hour a day." As for writing an effective goal for becoming rich and famous in Hollywood, when you figure that out, let me know.

Measurable

You should establish both short-term objectives and concrete benchmarks for measuring your progress toward the attainment of each goal. If you can't measure your progress, it will be impossible to know whether you are getting closer to achieving your goal. Being able to measure your advancement helps you to keep on track, maintain your focus, and reach completion dates. Likewise, each victory is cause for minicelebrations, and those joyous feelings associated with success motivate you to keep going and reach your goal.

In order to determine how your goal is measurable, you must establish qualitative criteria. Ask yourself questions like: How often will I do this? How much and how many? What will need to happen before I know my goal has been accomplished?

You may say you'd like to live healthier, but how is that measured specifically? You need to provide concrete and measureable evidence to this end. Examples of a healthier lifestyle that can be measured might include eating vegetables twice a day and fatty foods once a week, quitting smoking, and running on a treadmill for thirty minutes a day. If it is your dream to start your own business, an intermediate goal may be to cut expenses in order to save seed money. You can measure your progress (or lack thereof) by setting a measureable goal of a 10 percent reduction of expenses in two years' time.

Acceptable

When I say "acceptable," I'm referring to what is acceptable in the eyes of the Lord. Your goals and any method you employ to reach them should not be in conflict with what the Word of God teaches. Your goals should be not only for your higher good but also for the good of anyone they impact. The end does not justify the means. Just because your dream is God given does not mean you should go against God's Word in order to accomplish that dream. If you win at the expense of the Lord, you ultimately lose. Jesus asks, "What good is it for someone to gain the whole world, yet forfeit their soul?" (Mark 8:36).

Before you go too far down the wrong path, I suggest you make sure your plans for success don't violate biblical principles. Get alone with God and pray. Run your plans by a member of your clergy or a fellow believer further along his or her spiritual path than you. Please don't misunderstand me; you should make plans, but plans that don't consider God are plans destined to fail. The sensible alternative is found in James 4:15: "Instead, you ought to say, 'If it is the Lord's will, we will live and do this or that.'"

Realistic

No one is saying you should go out of your way to make things easy on yourself, but if you set your goals too high, then you run the risk of becoming overwhelmed and will more than likely give up. On the other hand, if you aim too low, you won't be challenged and you'll find the adventure boring and unrewarding—and you'll quit just the same.

Challenge yourself, but at the same time have realistic expectations. Goals should stretch you, but not beyond the breaking point. They should invite you to roam beyond your comfort zone and, in doing so, expose you to new achievements and maybe even unexpected destinations.

I had unrealistic goals when I first came to Los Angeles, and they almost sent me home. I wasn't able to make any real progress until I broke up my dream into realistically doable goals. Sadly, this would not happen for many years to come, and I suffered for it.

Timely = Deadlines

There is no way around it; we must ground our goals within a time frame and set deadlines. If we don't have a deadline in place, then we possess no urgency to start today and no clear sense of when our goal should be completed. A time-bound goal provides that sense of urgency, and a commitment to a deadline reinforces efforts to complete the goal on or before the due date.

Deadlines force you to move beyond the dreaming stage and kick-start you into actually doing something. Without deadlines, goals are not really goals at all; they're only wishes and flights of fancy.

But goals alone are not enough.

A MEANS TO AN END

When I painted houses during that summer in high school, the task before me was broken up into smaller minitasks. First, tape off the area you want to paint. Check. Then use a brush to paint the cutouts around the edges and the trim. Check. Last, use a roller to do the main field of the wall. Check. Repeat for every room in the house. Check, check. Without an overarching agenda or a master plan, however, I could easily end up painting a room the wrong color.

My point? If you only have goals but no dreams, you can easily fall into the trap of focusing so much on the steps that you lose sight of your destination. It's critical that you set goals, SMART or otherwise, in order to achieve your dream, *but goals alone won't always cut it*. Specific, short-term goals are not terribly motivating; their power comes from their connection to a big, inspiring dream.

If you focus solely on each individual step, one after the other, you may lose your place and not notice you are traveling in a circle. In addition, you might also fail to notice unexpected opportunities or shortcuts that would allow you to advance several steps ahead. When you keep your eye on your dream, it helps you to be on the lookout for those wonderful opportunities that may not seem to be aligned with your present goals but that strongly support your dream.

Goal setting is a process that involves a focused vision of what you want and a clear understanding of why you want it, including a series of well-defined intermediate steps that increase your odds for success. Always envision goals that are relatable to your dream, because without this focus you can end up with too many goals and not enough time to devote to each one. And remember that a goal is simply a means to an end, not the end in and of itself.

For behind-the-scenes photos of David's early acting years in Hollywood, including his first few roles on TV, visit DavidARWhite .com/Exclusive.

CHAPTER 4

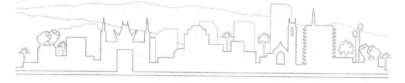

God Wants You to Succeed—Sometimes

Failure doesn't mean God has abandoned you, it just means God has a better idea.

John Maxwell

The series I was going to audition for was named *Evening Shade*. I remember thinking it was an odd name for a television show. I discovered later the name referred to a tiny town in Arkansas that was so called due to the shade offered by the many tall pines populating the area. Hillary Clinton, whose husband, William Clinton, was Arkansas' governor at the time, suggested the name to the producers of the show.

Evening Shade stood out from other shows on the air at the time because of its unprecedented high-profile—and very expensive—dream cast assembled mostly by Burt Reynolds. The cast was comprised of megastars from film and theater the likes of which had never before gathered to appear in a weekly TV show. Led by Burt, himself a veteran of over forty films and a former box-office champ, the show also featured Tony Award winners Charles Durning, Michael Jeter, and Elizabeth Ashley, five-time Emmy award-winning Hal Holbrook, film veteran Ossie Davis, and Marilu Henner, who had guest starred on the hit show *Taxi* for five years.

I, on the other hand, was fresh off the turnip truck from Kansas and was sleeping in a kitchen owned by a guy I met in a public restroom. So, yeah, I was pretty stoked about this audition, even if it was for just a role as an extra.

My first meeting with Burt Reynolds was a little anticlimactic. Burt gathered a group of teenaged guys who looked exactly like me and asked us a lot of seemingly trivial questions. Have you ever played football before? Were you an athlete in school? That kind of thing. We answered yes and shook our heads as if we were all captains of our varsity teams. (I was relieved that he didn't ask us to dance.)

I was lucky to get hired as what is called a "featured extra," which meant I was still a background player, but this time my face would be in focus. I didn't have any lines, but I would be on set with Burt Reynolds. I was thrilled to get the part.

A STAR IS BORN

On my first day of the job, I had a scene with Jay Ferguson, the young actor who played Taylor Newton, Burt Reynolds's son in the show. The episode was called "Something to Hold Onto," the eighth in the show's debut season. The premise for the story was that the high school football team needed to pass their algebra exams in order to play in that week's big game against the archrival town of Piggot. I was playing the part of one of the boys who made up the team. At the end of the episode, Burt asks us how we did on the algebra exam.

I wasn't supposed to say *anything* because I had no lines in this scene. I was only supposed to raise my hand, but for reasons I cannot explain, I spontaneously blurted out, "I got a B, Coach!" The other actors in the scene were stunned at what I had just done. An extra simply does *not* ad-lib during a scene. It's an egregious breach of protocol and, frankly, professionally very stupid. If you are able to watch the episode on DVD or YouTube, you can see how several of the actors literally pulled me back in line in case the director or one of the producers threw something at me for ad-libbing. Burt Reynolds, however, didn't miss a beat and simply responded, saying, "Good work, Philpott."

Philpott? Where did Burt come up with Philpott? The origin of the name aside, when Burt called me Philpott he was *naming* my character. Extras aren't supposed to have a name; that's why they're referred to as *extras*. The instant a character is named, the actor who plays that character goes from being an extra or featured player to guest star or costar. For the rest of the episode, Burt and then Michael Jeter continually referred to me as Philpott.

It's difficult for me to explain how rare and unorthodox this was. Consequently, the producers didn't know what to do with this development, and to this day neither my character's name nor mine is listed in the end credits for that episode.

Not bad for a kid who just a few days before was using a friend's refrigerator lamp as a night-light.

IN A TOWN CALLED EVENING SHADE

As it turned out, Burt Reynolds asked for me to appear in the show three more times during their first season, and my character rose up the ranks to what is called a recurring character. That is one step away from series regular, or to say it simply, having your own sitcom. Not only that, I was referred to as Philpott (and given the first name Andrew) for the next three seasons of *Evening Shade*.

For whatever reason, Burt Reynolds took a liking to me, often referring to me as "his discovery." He asked the writers of the show to include me as often as they could. As I said before, *Evening Shade* was a unique television show featuring some of the biggest names in show business either as series regulars or guest stars. Burt would just pick up the phone and ask any one of his legendary friends to come down for the week to share a few laughs and reminisce over old times. He played host to the likes of Tony Bennett, Bob Denver, Reba McEntire, Kenny Rogers, Leslie Nielsen, Richard Simmons, Robert Urich, Terry Bradshaw, Diahann Carroll, and John Ritter, to name a few. Then of course there were all the actors I had the chance to work with who weren't huge at the time but soon would be, like Billy Bob Thornton, Leah Remini, Scott Wolf, and two-time Academy Award winner Hilary Swank, who played my girlfriend. It was an honor to work with this caliber of professional actors, and I admit I was a bit starstruck.

No matter what time of day Burt's wife, Loni Anderson, dropped by the set, she was always done up and looking radiant. I should mention that Hollywood is a "kissy" town. That is to say, people often greet each other with a kiss. I was kissed by some of the most legendary and beautiful women in Hollywood during my tenure at *Evening Shade*. I got kisses and hugs from Loni, Raquel Welch, Marilu Henner, and many others.

In addition to all of the beautiful women Burt worked with and knew, there was also the obvious wealth he had acquired.

He and Loni each drove a brand new Mercedes-Benz. Once when I was sitting with him in his dressing room, his assistant came in and gave Burt $5,000 in cash to "get him through the weekend." Back in those days, $5,000 would have gotten me through the *year*.

But what impressed me most was that Burt was centered in this community, that he belonged there. I've already mentioned that my family moved around quite a bit. Every six years we found ourselves in a new town, a new church, and a new community. I had always wanted to plant roots, to stay in one place long enough to foster the kind of friendships that Burt had. I envied his ability to surround himself at any given moment with the people he most admired and respected.

I didn't realize it at the time, but the three seasons I spent with Burt Reynolds left an indelible mark on me. It's not surprising; after all, I met him when I was a very impressionable nineteen-year-old kid from Kansas and a struggling actor with just six months in Hollywood. He had success in his chosen field, respect from his peers, good friends, a whole lot of money, and a beautiful wife. Burt became my model for Hollywood success. He had everything I thought I wanted.

Over the three years that I knew him, Burt evolved into a Hollywood father figure to me on set. I looked up to him and sought his approval as much as any boy does from his dad. My dream of Hollywood changed after meeting Burt Reynolds, or perhaps I should say it was refined a bit. I wanted to be the guy who could hire his friends of twenty years to come and "play." I wanted to support and nurture young talent like Burt had done with me. No longer did I aspire to be simply a working actor in television and film. I wanted to produce, direct, be a star in

Hollywood. God, on the other hand, had different thoughts on the matter. Stay with me . . .

SUCCESS BREEDS SUCCESS

It's a funny thing about success in Hollywood. The minute you get some, more just seems to pour in. My life changed almost immediately after I finished my first episode of *Evening Shade*. Word got out that I had booked a recurring role on the show, and suddenly people were curious. They wanted to know who David A.R. White was.

During that three-year period, what I call my "milk and honey years," I booked several guest-starring appearances on TV shows such as *Coach*, *Melrose Place*, *Sisters,* and a made-for-TV movie called *Honor Thy Mother*. I also got my first starring role in a Christian film called *Second Glance*, which was directed by Christian filmmaker Rich Christiano. And don't even get me started on the commercials! I did Charmin commercials with the legendary Mr. Whipple, lots of different car commercials, several Maxwell House commercials, and an American Express commercial with Jerry Seinfeld that lasted eight years. But I was most excited about the two commercials I did with Cindy Crawford for the Pepsi "Gotta Have It" campaign that aired during the Super Bowl. These were all national ads paying top-dollar residuals each time they aired.

NEVER LET SUCCESS GO TO YOUR HEAD

There are two stereotypes of people who move to Hollywood in search of a dream: those whose dreams and souls are shattered in defeat, and those who get lucky and suddenly find themselves unprepared for success and implode. Both are equally debilitating and self-destructive. People who don't know how to handle their newfound fortune often live a life of excess. It's the whole "fast cars and faster women" scenario that ends in drug and alcohol addiction, disease, and even death.

By the grace of God, I was neither of these two tropes. In many respects I was still the same person I was in Kansas. Even though I was making more money than I had ever seen, I continued to live responsibly and frugally. While I was able to move out of Brian's kitchen and into my own place, I split the rent with several roommates. I ditched the motorcycle for a more practical form of transportation. Okay, that last one is not entirely true. I bought a Mustang. I wasn't Gandhi. I was nineteen! What did you expect?

My feet remained firmly planted on the ground and in my faith during those three years. I joined a church in Los Angeles and continued to attend faithfully. I didn't forget who I was or where I came from. I had not forfeited my morals or compromised my beliefs. Nor did I neglect to thank God for all the blessings he had given me, because I knew he was the source of my good fortune and he was the strength I was drawing from.

Which is why it was all the more painful when God allowed it all to be taken away.

NEVER LET FAILURE GO TO YOUR HEART

My success ended as abruptly as it started. It was toward the end of season three when we did an episode on *Evening Shade* where the kids in the cast were to imitate the townspeople in a high school play. Burt had chosen me to portray his character alongside Hilary Swank playing the role of my wife.

Burt had put on some weight as a result of some pain

medication he was taking, and I asked him if he thought it would be funny if I stuck a pillow under my shirt to mimic his swollen belly. Burt laughed and said, "Sure." The hair and makeup department went to work on me until I looked as much like Burt Reynolds as possible with hair, mustache, same wardrobe, and a big fat pillow.

The night we taped the episode, Burt introduced us all to the audience and he saved my introduction for last. I came out to greet the audience in my wig, mustache, and pillow. I did my Burt Reynolds impression and the crowd roared with laughter. I was in heaven. This was what I was meant to do.

Burt was smiling as he put his arm around me, which made me feel great, but then he smacked my ear really hard in such a way that no one else could see what he had done. It was obviously a move he had perfected, because afterwards Jay Ferguson nodded knowingly to me and said, "It really hurts, doesn't it?"

I did one more episode because it had already been written, but after that I was never asked to appear on *Evening Shade* again. My manager told me she had heard through the grapevine that I had offended Burt and that my services were no longer desired.

I felt horrible because the last thing I wanted to do was offend the man who had done so much for me, the man I looked up to like my Hollywood father. A few weeks later, I managed to arrange a meeting with Burt in his dressing room. We spoke for about forty-five minutes, and he assured me it was no big deal and that the producers had just decided to stop using the kids in the show so much. We shook hands, he wished me well, and I was sure I would neither see nor speak to Burt Reynolds again.

Actress Felicity Kendal is quoted as saying, "Success breeds success and failure leads to a sort of fallow period." I can attest to this as well. The end of my time on *Evening Shade* signaled the end of my three-year period of milk and honey. I was no longer asked to guest star on TV shows and was back to playing roles like room service waiter on *Melrose Place* and usher on a little show called *California Dreams*. Soon I was no longer asked to do even that.

Even the commercials began to dry up. It was hard to believe that just a few months earlier I had been working with Cindy Crawford, Regis Philbin, and John Tesh selling Pepsi on a national level and now—nothing. I wasn't prepared for it to end so fast, and I didn't understand why God would have let it happen. After all, I was living a solid, clean Christian life—one of abstinence, prayer, and devotion to God. How could he allow me to fail like this? Why did he give me a taste of my dream only to take it away? I was disappointed and confused. I wasn't angry, just a little scared about what the future would bring.

The anger would come later.

It may seem strange that a book that claims that God wants us all to succeed in his plans for us would devote an entire chapter to failure. The idea that God may allow his children to fail is counter to much of what you may have heard in some of those feel-good "God Wants You to Have a Brand New Car!" books or during one of your favorite televised sermons. Oftentimes we Christians believe we are entitled to a lifetime of undefeated seasons. We think each of our whims and desires should all be granted.

I've seen it before. Many believers think they are somehow

exempt or immune to failure because of their relationship with Jesus. *I know this to be true because I was one of them.*

I used to repeat Psalm 37:4 day in and day out while I imagined my success in Hollywood. I still believe the verse to be true, except now I think the Lord knows the desires of our hearts better than we do. God may have different plans or desires than we ever thought we wanted, and his plans are more gratifying. Consider a mother's relationship with her child. The child truly believes a $3,000 pair of Gold-Dipped Nike Dunks will bring immeasurable long-term happiness, but Mom knows the euphoria associated with such a purchase will have a limited shelf life. She knows that there are far more spiritually and emotionally rewarding experiences later in the child's future. Finally, Mom knows that no pair of sneakers is worth $3,000. Just saying.

There are going to be times in your life, most probably during your quest for dream fulfillment, when you are going to experience a failure. Your knee-jerk reaction might be to blame God or to feel that somehow he has shorted you, but the truth is, he is not the cause of our failures, although he does allow them from time to time and for a variety of reasons.

NO EXCEPTIONS

God never says that we won't encounter problems, sorrow, or failure just because we believe in him. As a matter of fact, Job 14:1 tells us, "Mortals, born of woman, are of few days and full of trouble." Life is full of trouble for *everyone*. This truth is not one that applies only to the "ungodly" or to "unbelievers," but to every person born into this world. While this is not the kind of thing you're going to see hanging on an inspirational poster at a motivational speaker's conference, God has included it in his

Word. He wants us to know that we should expect life to stink sometimes, even for those of us who belong to God through faith in Christ.

I want to have a discussion about failure in a Christian's life because it's so rarely talked about, leaving many believers spiritually unprepared when it happens to them. Many Christians simply aren't prepped to face or to deal with failure, and therefore the experience can be debilitating, and the questions it raises can be very disheartening: *Where was God when I needed him most? How did he let this happen to me? Did I do something wrong? Is God angry with me? Does God really exist?*

TWO KINDS OF FAILURE

There's a difference between someone who *fails as a Christian* and a *Christian who fails.* I know it sounds like hair-splitting semantics, but it's not.

Failing as a Christian refers to failure in a believer's relationship and walk with God. This is the kind of thing we are warned about in Sunday school as kids and from the pulpit as adults.

This kind of failure comes when you ignore God's commandments or allow yourself to be led astray by temptations. You've basically dug your own grave with a shovel called "sin." Failure of this type is, for the most part, a spiritual dilemma, a matter of moral, ethical, and spiritual failure.

The second type of failure is less about spiritual matters and has more to do with things that go wrong in the life of a Christian. It is not dependent upon or necessarily related to sin in the life of the believer. Christians can fail even when they are following God's commands and fleeing temptation. For example, a Christian farmer might lose his farm because for several years in a row his crops are decimated by blight. A Christian ballerina might watch her dreams go up in flames when she fails to be selected for the American Ballet Theatre—and a Christian actor might watch his career come to a screeching halt when he has unintentionally offended the person who was helping him in Hollywood.

Christians go bankrupt, become unemployed, get divorced, and have their hearts broken for any number of reasons. Many times we cannot connect the dots between these episodes of failure and a pattern of sin in our lives. Our "days are full of trouble." Sometimes because of sin actions, and sometimes not.

This kind of failure can be more unsettling and have greater consequences than the first because it takes us off guard. We don't know how to properly respond to it. I know I didn't. I spent many nights confused and frustrated, asking, "Why me, Lord?" I was living a good, obedient, and clean Christian life. I was going to church, witnessing when appropriate, and praying regularly. I had not fallen into the pit of drugs and promiscuous sex, like so many of my peers. So when the acting jobs came to an end, I wondered, *How could a walk down the path of righteousness put me on the road to failure?*

PERSECUTION IS NOT FAILURE

We are assured that "Blessed are you when people insult you, persecute you and falsely say all kinds of evil against you because of me. Rejoice and be glad, because great is your reward in heaven, for in the same way they persecuted the prophets who were before you" (Matthew 5:11–12).

When I speak of failure, I'm not talking about episodes of Christian persecution. History is full of examples of Christians being persecuted for living godly lives in Jesus Christ. Sadly, you can find similar examples of Christian persecution and discrimination in today's news headlines, but these are not cases of genuine failure. If a Christian loses his job, for instance, because of his Christian worldview, then it's hardly appropriate to say he failed. As a matter of fact, according to the aforementioned Scripture from Matthew, God will bless him or her for it!

We also need to differentiate failure from *trials*. I'll talk more about this later, but for now it's important to differentiate trials from failure. The apostle Peter tells us that trials are an inevitable facet of the Christian experience, and they serve the purpose of testing our Christian growth, endurance, and maturity (1 Peter 4:12–13).

Persecution and trials aside, why does it sometimes appear that God calls one of his obedient children, places a dream in that child's heart, but then allows that child to fail? I've come to only one conclusion.

A SHOCKING TRUTH: GOD MAY ALLOW YOU TO FAIL

I wonder how many of you just threw this book into the garbage can. Take a breath, maybe get yourself a glass of water, and when you're ready, we'll continue.

I grew up with the firm belief that any believer who was walking in God's will could not fail in the pursuit of his God-given appointment. After being in Los Angeles for only six months I had already found work on a hit sitcom with one of Hollywood's biggest stars, making five times per week what my father was earning. I felt like I was golden, like God was blessing me beyond all others. I thought of myself as the poster boy for "whatever they do prospers" (Psalm 1:3). I considered myself a walking testimonial for "I will do whatever you ask in my name" (John 14:13). Although I was enormously grateful to the Lord for my relatively instant success, I was not at all surprised by it.

Watching it all evaporate with similar speed, however, knocked the wind out of me. I was brokenhearted, ashamed, and humiliated. I was confused and frustrated. My dad would have probably told me easy come, easy go, and to remember that money isn't everything.

HOW GOD USES FAILURE

For some of us, failure can be a way in which God gets our attention. It's a tap on the shoulder in an effort to get us to come back to him if we have wandered away and gone astray. Sometimes that tap can be a painful experience that he uses to express his fatherly love.

For others, failure can serve as a reminder that we cannot live a truly Christian life on our own, independent of God. At times the Lord will put us in a scenario that will convince us we are inadequate, so that we don't try to go it alone. He uses failure to remind us that we need to depend more on him.

Looking back, I believe that God allowed me to experience failure because *there were lessons I needed to learn that I could not have learned through success.* But it took awhile for me to understand this, and I don't want to get ahead of my story, so you'll have to wait for a later chapter to find out what those lessons were! The next time you fail, you might ask yourself if the Lord might have allowed you to fail in order to ready you for something completely different, and this "something" might only be achieved through failure.

It's quite possible that if I had not experienced failure and had continued without a glitch on that road to "success," I would not be where I am today in either my life or my spiritual walk. This is because at twenty-two years of age, I had no idea of what true success was. I believed then, as I do today, that God had placed a dream in my heart, but the Lord and me, well, we had different ideas of what living that dream was going to look like. I was dreaming of swimming pools, movie star friends, and massive paydays. The Lord? Not so much. I believe God allowed me to fail because he knew that was the only way I would *eventually* "change lanes" and see things his way.

Is this a different way of looking at failure for you? It's been convicting and encouraging for me to realize that my failure may be considered a success in the greater scheme of things and in the eyes of God. This understanding has changed the way I look at failure. When we see how God uses failure, we begin to see it as our friend rather than our enemy—as something we should welcome and go through rather than avoid or deny.

Sometimes failure is an *opportunity* to respond with courage and faithful dependency as opposed to anger, despondency, or rebellion.

YOU MAY NEVER KNOW WHY . . . SO WHAT?

It goes without saying that we should try to learn from our failures and determine if there is a lesson God is trying to teach us. I encourage you, however, not to get too hung up on why God allowed you to fail. I know it is part of human nature to try to unravel the "why" of things. I consider this unrelenting curiosity one of humankind's greatest strengths, but we have to accept that when it comes to the mind and sovereignty of God, we may never know why some things happen. It's pointless to spend sleepless nights, tossing and turning, trying to understand why God allowed this or that terrible misfortune to enter our lives. We don't have to understand why it happened in order to benefit from it.

Instead, ask yourself, how should I have behaved in the situation? Or how will I act differently the next time? Consider how God would have wanted you to behave and respond. Ask how you have been strengthened by the ordeal and how you are now better prepared to move forward. At the time, I didn't realize the wisdom of looking at failure this way, and therefore I internalized it. This is another example of *don't make the mistakes I made*. I didn't ask myself these questions and instead allowed the experience to beat me up for years to come.

DON'T QUIT

Everyone is going to fail from time to time, but you are only considered a "failure" when you allow failure to defeat you. You are only a failure when you give up and refuse to try again. Remember, there is a difference between failing and being a failure.

Henry Ford had five businesses that failed and left him broke before he founded the Ford Motor Company. Walt Disney was fired from a newspaper for "not being creative enough," and Elvis Presley was told at his Grand Ole Opry audition to "go back to driving a truck."

It is not God's master plan that we become failures. This would make Christianity a very unpopular religion. There are times, however, when God will allow us to fail today so that we might succeed tomorrow. Deep within your failure are planted the roots of your success.

Failure, in varying degrees, is inevitable along the path to dream fulfillment. So when you fail, don't despair or think God has abandoned you. Take comfort in knowing failure doesn't mean you're finished. You're only finished if you quit. Ask for God's strength to continue, and allow him to build within you the endurance you're going to need in order to live the dream he has planted in your heart. Every hardship you endure, every failure you withstand, could very well be a stepping-stone to success and the realization of your dreams. Try to maintain a positive perspective. Don't spend years of your life wallowing in hopelessness. Try not to become bitter and angry. In other words, don't do what I did.

To see David working with Burt Reynolds, Terry Bradshaw, Hilary Swank, and other stars of the hit TV series Evening Shade, *go to DavidARWhite.com/Exclusive.*

CHAPTER 5

The Hard Part

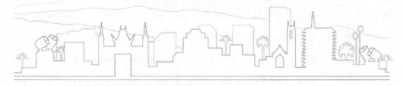

*Hardships often prepare ordinary
people for extraordinary destiny.*

C. S. Lewis

C ar stereo theft was a crime that plagued automobile owners throughout the 1990s. Back in those days, the factory-installed stereos were garbage, so many of us upgraded with aftermarket stereos. Oftentimes, these stereos could be removed and carried around on your person in order to deter theft. I had such a stereo that I would literally carry in my jacket pocket, and that is what I was doing on the night I was mugged.

A few years after my time on *Evening Shade,* while I was still wallowing in the bottomless fallow that had become my life, I walked out of a theater located off of Hollywood Boulevard and Ivar Avenue where I was performing in a play. Two men approached me rather threateningly and one of them demanded, "Give me your stereo." The other man placed his hand inside his jacket to signify that he was armed.

My reaction was uncharacteristic of me. Normally I am levelheaded. Under typical circumstances I would have done the smart and prudent thing and simply handed over the stereo and considered myself lucky that was all I lost. But at that moment, my life was already in shambles. It had been several years since I had any meaningful employment. Both my savings and prospects for the future were dwindling fast. I was entering my midtwenties, but I considered myself a has-been. I felt very much like the title character from the movie *Wyatt Earp* when he said, "Mister, I've been in a really bad mood for the last few years, so I'd appreciate it if you'd just leave me alone."

Of course I didn't say anything nearly as cool as that. I think I managed to squeeze out a meager, "What?" I couldn't believe I was being robbed. I saw his hand in his pocket, hoped that it wasn't a gun, and felt the guy behind me. But, I have to say, I didn't care. I wasn't about to hand over my stereo. And so I replied, "No." But that *no* was infused with three years of anger, bitterness, and despair. As no's go, it was pretty definitive.

I'm guessing that's why one of them punched me in the face.

I'm sure these muggers thought punching me in the face would be the last word, and it probably should have been. But instead, I did the thing police recommend you never do: I punched the guy back. I fought back and wrestled with these two guys, not so much because the stereo was important to me, but rather because I was so angry—at God and at the state of my life. "How dare you," was all I could think. The injustice of it all left me incredulous.

After a brief scuffle, the two ran off in one direction, and I escaped to another. They never got my radio, but I got a black eye. It would not be the last time I was roughed up for standing up for myself.

HARD TIMES

Over the next few years, I continued to do the odd commercial here and there and managed to get very small roles in some very small television shows like *Saved by the Bell: The College Years.* The money was just enough to keep me afloat, but my savings were dwindling fast.

In an effort to cut back, I left the house I was living in and got a cheaper one with one of my old roommates.

I probably spent a good year in denial about my employment prospects. My peers, the people I hung around with back in the *Evening Shade* days, were all still pursuing their careers in acting and doing well. I told myself, "You're just going through a dry spell. Just hang in for a while longer and soon you'll be enjoying the same success as Scott Wolf, Hilary Swank, and Leo DiCaprio." (By the way, if I failed to mention this earlier, Leo used to hang out on our set while he was young and on *Growing Pains*.) I told myself we were all living the dream, but that there were different levels and that for now, at least temporarily, my peers inhabited a level different from my own.

It's a wonderfully positive attitude, but you can't pay the rent with it. I finally took whatever odd jobs I could find. I was a waiter at Pizza Hut and worked in an AT&T call center for several months. When people who worked with me asked me where I came from and what I had been up to, no one believed that I was an actor and had been on television, that I had worked with Burt Reynolds and Cindy Crawford, or that I had starred in a movie. After a while, I stopped telling people. After a while, I began to question it myself.

My job situation went from bad to bizarre.

TWISTS AND TURNS, OBSTACLES AND DETOURS

It's difficult for an actor to take a mainstream job with normal nine-to-five working hours because you must remain available for auditions and readings that occur during that same period. After all of the waiter and waitress jobs are spoken for, an actor must get resourceful and think outside of the box. However, you must be careful not to let anyone know how low in the barrel you've had to scrape because Hollywood is a town all about perception, and the folks here avoid desperation like the plague.

A friend of mine who owned a party company said he had an easy way for me to make a hundred dollars for an hour's work. "Just one hour," he told me. "It will be the easiest hundred dollars of your life." I drove down to his shop that day without really thinking it through. I know, shocker, right?

My buddy was thrilled to see me. Apparently he was having a hard time finding someone to fill this particular job. "What's the job?" I asked.

The next thing I knew, I was dressed in a full Barney the Dinosaur suit. I was scheduled to arrive at a seven-year-old girl's birthday party already wearing the suit. I was told it would be considered unprofessional if I put the costume on once I was at the venue. I guess it ruins the magic of the moment if the children see you getting dressed. I wasn't sure I could drive safely dressed like a purple dinosaur, but a hundred dollars is a hundred dollars, so I was willing to try.

"How far do I have to drive?" I asked.

My friend shifted on his feet for a moment and then sheepishly replied, "Well, that's kind of the thing. You have to go into Compton."

Compton is situated in southern Los Angeles County, and in the 1990s it was considered one of the ten most dangerous cities in America, home to the Bloods and Crips, two rival gangs continually at war with one another. This is where I was headed—dressed from head to toe in a purple felt Barney suit. I had walked through Cabrini-Green in Chicago in the middle of the night; how bad could this be, right?

I parked my car in front of the customer's house, put on my Barney head, and then walked across the street to the front door. The birthday girl answered my knock and matter-of-factly informed me that I was an hour early. Her uncle then invited me to join him on the couch and watch a football game until the party got under way. I looked at my options. There was a gang standing on the street corner watching me, so I figured watching football would be the safer of the two.

Picture the scene: Barney the Dinosaur sharing a bowl of stale potato chips with a middle-aged man wearing a tank top and complaining about new regulations in college football. If that makes you feel awkward, then you know how I was feeling. But it gets better.

A bit later the girl came over to me, peered through the mesh of my Barney helmet, which of course I was still wearing, and whispered, "I know you're not real. You can take your Barney head off." Even though it's considered an egregious breach of costumed character etiquette to remove your headpiece while on the job, I figured the jig was up, so I finished watching the game without my head. The afternoon ended with no further incident other than my bruised ego. The family actually tipped me despite the fact that I had not memorized the Barney song. Somehow that only made me feel worse.

The same friend who set me up with the Barney gig later hired me to dress as a court jester and hand out flyers at an antique art sale. I've never figured out what a kingly court's fool and antique art have in common, but I took the job because I needed the money.

I arrived with literal bells on and began handing out flyers to all of the upscale customers such an event would attract, until I heard my name being called. "David. David, is that you?"

I turned to the voice and to my horror discovered it was a very high-profile casting director from one of the major studios in town. The very same casting person who had placed me in so many of the television shows I had done just a year or two ago. I think we were both embarrassed to have run into each other. When she asked, "How are you?" I wanted to say, "I'm dressed as a court jester handing out flyers to rich people who are here to buy old stuff. How do you think I am?" I think I said instead, "Terrific!" She smiled and left me there to finish out the job. She never hired me again.

I never knew what the next day would bring. After three years of wandering, taking any job I could get, and struggling just to keep my head above water, I began to forget why I had come to Hollywood in the first place. I wasn't advancing toward my dream or making any progress. I was treading water in this whirlpool that every day threatened to swallow me up. My immediate short-term goal was to make enough money to live, but even that was getting more difficult by the day. I took my eyes off the dream, the *big picture,* and concentrated only on the demands of the day. Without the inspiration of an overarching dream, I began to just exist.

God-given dreams fuel and motivate you, but I had unplugged myself from my dream and was now sputtering on life support. My passive involvement in my life only served to make things worse. I was depressed, resented my hardships, and spent too much time feeling sorry for myself and struggling with why God had allowed this to happen to me. I did little to make things better in my life, and that in turn only exacerbated the problem. I thought about going home, but then remembered I had no home to go back to. My parents were still in Canada, and I just didn't see a place there for me. So I wandered and was knocked around like a pinball in an arcade game.

Looking back, I realize only now that I was in another wheat field of sorts, cursing one life and wishing for another. In hindsight, I bet God was trying to tell me something, but I was just too miserable to hear. I was about to learn the lengths God would take to get my attention.

FROM BAD TO WORSE

Not long after I hit hard times in my career, I met Christy, the woman who would become my first real girlfriend. I wasn't planning on falling in love. Whoever does? It wasn't the best time in my life for a romantic pursuit, considering I was going through so many transitions and was so strapped financially.

I was with a buddy of mine at a Los Angeles production of *A Chorus Line*. At the time I was not a fan of musical theater. I've since changed my opinion, but back then I considered the whole thing a massive yawn. Nevertheless, I found myself watching this show and then later went backstage to say hello to some friends. That's where I first laid eyes on Christy, a singer and dancer in the show.

Christy and I hit it off almost immediately. We spent three great years together. For much of that time, I believed she was "the one" and that we would eventually marry. Her parents, however, did not share my optimistic view of their only child's future. They never believed I was good enough for Christy, and the fact that I was broke and struggling to find work didn't make things any better.

Christy was a great girl, and all of my friends loved her, but toward the end of our relationship we fought more than we did anything else. I wanted to get married, but she maintained that her career came first, so she kept delaying the decision. Her parents had drilled it into her head that all else in her life could wait until she had a solid career. It didn't help that I had to dress up like Barney in order to get through the tough times. We argued about that too. She thought that kind of work was beneath me. But I had bills to pay. I figured that as long as a job was legal and didn't offend the Lord, I would do what I had to do. It also didn't help that Christy was on the road a lot, performing around the country, which meant that we were apart a great deal of the time. (Looking back, I wonder if that's why we lasted as long as we did.)

I think I held on to our relationship so long because it was the only thing I had left that resembled stability. Despite that, I had begun to realize I would never marry her, and so on the anniversary of our third year together, I told her I could not see her anymore. We were both devastated. I took it hard because, despite the fact that I had invested three years into the relationship, it ended poorly. In many ways I considered it another failure to add to my growing list. I began to wonder if I wasn't good enough for her or for any woman, as her parents clearly believed.

I was getting used to the feeling of having it all and then losing it. I had been feeling this way for quite some time. I guess that's why I fought so hard for a cheap, removable stereo. I had been in a bad mood for the last few years.

Hard times.

I read somewhere on the Internet, "Hard times are like a washing machine. They twist, turn, and knock us around, but in the end we come out cleaner, brighter, and better than before." Right. Try telling that to a guy who has lost his job, his home, and the love of his life.

I could have stopped chasing my dream right then and there and no one would have blamed me. I was broke, both my bank account and my heart. To make things even more difficult, most of the people I knew in Kansas thought I was crazy for going to Hollywood in the first place. Whenever I spoke to them on the phone, a few relatives kept asking me how long was I going to keep "doing that Hollywood thing?" I could have decided my dream was simply a pipe dream. I could have quit and gone back to Moody, become a pastor, and married a nice church girl.

But I didn't. And I hope that when you encounter hard times, you don't either.

THE ROAD TO SUCCESS: A TANGLED BALL

Hold the two ends of a string in each of your hands and stretch it taut. Now raise your right hand so that the string travels in a forty-five-degree incline from left to right. That's how most people assume their path to success will look: a linear journey that with time and effort will steadily rise until their dream is fulfilled.

Now let me demonstrate what the path to success truly looks like. Take the very same string and tie it into knots. Throw it on the floor and walk all over it. Go outside and drag it through the mud. Kick it to the curb, run it through the mill, and beat it to a pulp.

Now look at the string. It should look like a tangled, messy knot, an overlapping, twisting ball of chaos. That's the true path to success and dream fulfillment. Look more closely at the string and study it carefully. See those scrambled loops? Those are called "second thoughts." And how about those tiny knots? They're "confusion." Notice the frayed and split ends, the parts of the string that were almost torn in two. Those are "hard times," those moments during your quest when you will be tempted to give up.

Don't try to unravel the string and straighten it out. Don't spend too much time staring at the string, trying to make sense of it. I say this because if you're planning to embark on the road to success, then you need to be prepared for the detours, roadblocks, and potholes you will inevitably encounter along the way.

While pursuing your God-given dream is one of the most rewarding and exciting things you'll ever do, it can also be very nerve-racking, frustrating, and challenging. When faced with a roadblock or detour, many people simply choose to give up. We quit on our dreams for a variety of reasons. You'll hear words and phrases like *settle, change of plans,* and *fizzled out.*

One of the saddest reasons for abandoning a dream I ever

heard was from a high school friend who dreamed of being a world-class athlete. He most certainly had what it takes, but when I ran into him years later, I learned that he had abandoned the goal. When I asked him why, he replied, "I just grew up."

A lot of people set out in life to pursue their dreams, but too few actually achieve them. They hit a snag, start to flounder, get lost, or just walk away. I don't want you to be one of those people, so let's take a look at some of the tough situations and circumstances you may come up against along your journey.

WHY SOME NEVER ACHIEVE THEIR GOD-GIVEN DREAM

There are five reasons some people never achieve their dreams: following their dream was harder than they thought, they suffer from indecision, they lack self-confidence, they are unwilling to adapt, and they face spiritual conflict.

Harder Than You Thought

"I had no idea it was going to be this tough." I chuckle when I hear this, especially from people wanting to make it in show business. If it were easy, everybody could do it. The same is true for whatever your dream involves. It's unlikely that your dream will be easy to obtain.

If you find yourself bogged down in hard times, if you feel that your dream pursuit has stalled, ask yourself if your expectations and goals are realistic. When I first started down the Yellow Brick Road, I thought I would be on my way to stardom the minute I stepped foot in Hollywood. Okay, that is kind of what happened initially, but I expected my success to grow, and when it diminished I was unprepared. As a result, those hard times knocked me back and kept me down. Do your research before you set out, adjust your expectations if need be, and above all have some patience.

Indecision

On the other hand, don't run out your clock trying to come up with the perfect plan before you do anything. That's just a cleverly disguised version of procrastination. Don't kid yourself into thinking you're doing something by doing nothing. Doing the wrong thing can sometimes be better than doing nothing at all because at least you can learn something from activity. Even a step in the wrong direction has its merits. Stop wasting time. Yes, have a plan. Yes, complete your due diligence, but don't stay stuck in this stage. At some point you're going to have to take a deep breath and leap!

Lack of Self-Confidence

I know people who have lost the race before it even started because their defeat was all in their heads. These people had talent and resources but lacked self-confidence. You shouldn't refuse to knock on a door just because you're afraid no one will open it. Trust in yourself the way God trusts in you. Get out of your own way and let God open some of those doors for you.

Unwilling to Adapt

Somewhere along the way you may discover the need to adjust or modify your plan for success, or even to tweak what your vision of success looks like in the first place. Remember, your first attempt at something is not your *only* attempt. Don't let your pride or stubbornness stop you from reevaluating your position and adapting as the situation demands. God may be asking that you change direction midstream.

Spiritual Conflict

The hard times you face may be a result of spiritual warfare you are battling. Much has been written on this topic, and it is beyond the scope of this book, but suffice it to say trials are meant to transform and shape you for the better, not cripple or destroy you.

I was stuck in this battle for a good three years and almost lost the fight, yielding to the enemy, because I lost my focus. Just because you're at a temporary standstill and lack forward momentum doesn't mean you have to lose ground and go backward. In her book *Starting Your Day Right*, Joyce Meyer writes, "You may not know how to forge ahead, but you can stand firmly on what you know of God."

WHY? WHY? WHY?

In the last chapter we talked about how failures are inevitable for all of us. Oftentimes the aftermath of failing, the debris that is left behind, includes trials and misfortunes—the hard times. Just as we can't avoid a natural storm, we can't avoid the storms of life. All we can do is prepare for them and learn to ride them out.

Meteorologists are scientists paid to figure out why storms form in the first place. They use words and concepts like "low-pressure areas," "latent heat/energy," and "conduction," all in an effort to explain the root causes for storms. Have you ever heard that you should do the same with respect to the storms that happen in your own life? You have probably been advised that in order to understand God's greater good for you, you should dig deep and uncover the reasons for the trials you experience.

I don't think this is a bad idea in and of itself; however, I caution you not to get stuck in this "Why me, Lord?" stage. I spent several years agonizing over the reason for my misfortune instead of dealing with the problems at hand. Was it a bad decision I made? Did I heed the wrong advice? Was it sin? Was I traveling down the wrong path and God was trying to redirect me?

My kids play these video games that have a "Map View" feature which allows the player to toggle back and forth between the player's limited view and a broad, bird's-eye view of the entire game. With a click, the player can see the whole universe he inhabits. He can see the hidden treasures and rewards, the precise locations of the bad guys, the direction everybody is moving, and potential hazards and detours. With this view, the player can see his own location with respect to everything else that is happening in the world of the game.

Now imagine a switch that would allow you to see not only this, but simultaneously all that has happened in the world since the beginning of time and the entirety of the future yet to happen. That's how God sees the world. He knows all that you have done, what you're doing, and the infinite possibilities of your future. For better or worse, we as mortals cannot share this "God's-Eye View" of the universe, and because we lack his divine omniscience, the reasons and causes for things are often not clear to us.

While I believe you should be introspective and spend time in prayer and seek godly counsel as to why you might be experiencing tough periods in your life, I want to say again that you may never get an answer as to the "why" of it all. There are times when the cause or reason just won't be obvious, and you may never know. The biblical character Job had a lot of setbacks, and as far as I can tell, he never found out the "why" of it all.

It may be that God doesn't want you to have all of the answers, or he feels you're not ready to hear or understand them. Whatever the case, don't get hung up or stuck looking for reasons. While you're wasting your time wallowing in misery, you place yourself at risk of missing the greater point and the lessons that your hard times were designed to teach you.

NO RAIN, NO RAINBOWS

Trials, troubles, and tribulations. Call them what you like; I prefer to just say "hard times." It will be highly unlikely for you to avoid these low spots along your journey to dream fulfillment. The only thing you have control over is how you react and respond when they happen.

"God is our refuge and strength, an ever-present help in trouble" (Psalm 46:1). God's opinion of hard times and troubles is not like ours. Where we see a crisis, jeopardy, and cause for depression, he sees opportunity for enrichment, spiritual growth, and an education toward our betterment. Try to redirect your thinking when faced with hard times so you can appreciate the opportunities presented through them, or you may miss the benefits God is trying to bestow on you.

Hard Times Reveal You

My son buys these toys in what they call "blind bags." They're little plastic sacks that conceal mini-themed toys. You can't see the toy inside until you open it up, and then SURPRISE! Sometimes problems and tribulations open us up before God. Think about a problem you've faced recently. How did you behave? Did you learn anything from it? What do you think is revealed about your character from how you face difficult situations? What is motivating and governing your behavior—your own self-serving desires, or is Christ the true Lord of your life? When we deal with problems the right way, it confirms our true identity as Christians.

Hard Times Improve You

I know you've heard it before: adversity builds character. Eleanor Roosevelt once said, "Do one thing every day that scares you." I always say you should try to push yourself to be comfortable in the uncomfortable.

Trials help to create a steadfast faith that will overcome, much in the way a marathon runner subjects his body to a torturous regime in order to endure the race. When we persevere through a trial, we become stronger spiritually. Without trials, we might abandon our Christian walk at the first sign of stomach cramps. Okay, maybe not the best analogy, but my point is that trials, tests, and hardships can strengthen us spiritually and are designed to bring us victoriously to the other side. As trite and commonplace as this may seem, it begins to make sense when you compare the process to building physical strength by lifting weights at the gym. For the exercise to pay off, you have to go beyond your comfort zone. You must push yourself a little more each day.

Bottom line: All of us need to be challenged in order to grow. As you successfully meet these obstacles and storms in your life, you build and strengthen your resiliency, making it easier for you to deal with the next challenge that comes along. God wants you to be physically and spiritually fit and is more interested in your character as a Christian than in whether your "muscles" are sore the next day.

Hard Times Train You

Sometimes—and sadly it's far too often—the only way to learn in life and to grow as human beings is by suffering and setbacks. I have three small children, and I tell them over and over again, "Don't." I tell them to be careful around this and to stay away from that. My children don't listen to me any better than I did to my parents. Hard-learned lessons often come with a price.

I once heard a stand-up comedian do a routine about how expensive it is to baby-proof a house and how his own father never did such a thing when he was a child. The comedian went on to say that his father actually once told him to put a metal fork into an electrical socket. After he was shocked, the father asked him, "You ever going to do that again?" The comedian tearfully answered, "No." The father nodded and declared the house baby-proofed.

God does not enjoy it when we suffer, but such is his love for us that he will resort to doing what he has to do for us to learn some tough lessons. Pain and suffering are a part of life. We have to accept it, expect it, and learn from it.

LOOK FORWARD

I think one of the saddest realities of the human condition is that oftentimes we only learn the value of something by losing it. But when that happens, we must move on and not dwell on it. There are going to be times in your life when you have to forget what is gone, be thankful for what you still have, and look forward to those things yet to come. The apostle Paul wrote, "Let the peace of Christ rule in your hearts, since as members of one body you were called to peace. And be thankful" (Colossians 3:15).

My point is best expressed by the apostle Paul in his letter to the Romans: "Not only so, but we also glory in our sufferings, because we know that suffering produces perseverance; perseverance, character; and character, hope" (5:3–4). When you go through hard times, remember that God is not picking on you. Even if you can't figure out why you're going through periods of adversity, trust that God has got your back. You're going to make it through the storm, and when you do, you'll be better and stronger.

To see David dressed for his gig as Barney the Purple Dinosaur, go to DavidARWhite.com/Exclusive.

CHAPTER 6

Time to Stop Talking and Start Listening

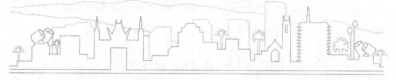

*God's dream for your life is more rewarding
than you've ever dreamed of. Now stay
open and let God do it his way.*

Unknown

I met the great actor and comedian Leslie Nielsen at a bank on the day I moved to Los Angeles. I asked him what I needed to do in order to succeed in Hollywood. He answered, "Perseverance, kid." His words resonated with me for many years after. I kept telling myself that all I had to do was stick it out, and my turn would come. I just needed to take more acting classes, meet more casting directors, sign with better agents, and do more theater.

While the idea of perseverance is certainly a wise if not noble concept, success in your God-given dream will usually require more than only a *stick-to-it* attitude. There was something missing in my recipe for success, an ingredient that had evaded me for almost a decade. We read in James 1:12, "Blessed is the one who perseveres under trial because, having stood the test, that person will receive the crown of life that the Lord has promised to those who love him." In both the New and Old Testaments the word *test* means to "prove by trial."

When God tests us, he is looking for us to prove that our faith is of substance. Of course, since God knows all things, he doesn't need proof for himself. He is proving to us and to those around us that our faith is strong and that our faith in him can withstand the storms of adversity and trial.

THE MAN IN THE MIRROR

Another few years had passed, and as I approached my thirties I was neither persevering nor was I particularly blessed. While I was hustling and trying to figure out why I wasn't moving any closer to seeing my dream fulfilled, my heart began to grow cold, and I grew further away from God. I was disappointed in him and felt that he had failed me.

Like most declines, mine happened gradually. It was a compromise here and a concession there. With each passing year of "failure," I surrendered a little more of the good fight: I stopped going to church regularly; I read my Bible less and less; I made no effort to stay connected with other believers; I dated non-believers and experimented with the usual Hollywood fare of illegal substances; I smoked and sometimes drank to excess.

If I had bothered to look at myself in the mirror, I wouldn't have recognized who I had become. But during this period, I didn't spend much time looking at my life. The last thing I wanted to do was face or confront myself. In many ways, I closed my eyes to much of what I was doing. Young people sometimes use their innocence as an excuse to be unwise. In many ways, this is what I was doing.

Primarily I felt a vacancy in my heart, like a piece of me was missing. I blamed any number of things for this: financial difficulties, a failed relationship, a struggling career. And while those issues certainly took their toll, I was mostly missing my true Mentor and Friend. Before coming to Hollywood, I had spent most of my life walking with God, and now that I had strayed from him, I felt a void that nothing on this earth could fill. While I realize all of this *now*, I didn't then, so I spent most of my time intensely frustrated and depressed. *What am I doing here? What have I just sacrificed the last ten years of my life for?*

At the core of my depression was my lack of purpose. I hadn't yet connected my dream to the fact that God had placed it in my heart because he had something special for me to do. That realization would come a bit later. For now I had no greater direction. I was a grown man, and yet I was living in a rented home with a bunch of roommates like some frat boy. I had let my parents down by not completing college and declining to enter the ministry. Both my girlfriend and her parents didn't think I was a safe bet for marriage. I had lost my connection to God and to the dream he had planted in me, and I had become unmoored in my walk. In many ways, my dream had defined me, and without it, I didn't know who I was anymore or what I was supposed to be doing with my life.

So I wandered further and further from the Lord. This wasn't a conscious decision. I didn't wake up one day and decide that I didn't need to obey God's laws anymore. I didn't question his existence.

For all of my teenage and young adult life I'd had this vision of what success in Hollywood would look like: I would make a lot of money, become a famous power player in Hollywood, and be friends with lots of other celebrities—all the while remaining true to my Christian beliefs and standards. Nothing short of this would be acceptable.

I'm embarrassed to admit this now, but I truly believed God was going to grant my dream—like he was some kind of genie out of its bottle. When he didn't, I was stumped, confused, and angry. I had many low points during this period, when I felt God had forgotten me. Of course he was there all along, trying to communicate with me, but my self-pity drowned him out. Instead of listening, I was too busy complaining and feeling sorry for myself.

Even so, God kept working behind the scenes to get me back on a firm spiritual path so that I could find my purpose and understand the fullness of the dream he had given me.

One day I went to see an old casting company that had hired me in all those high-profile and well-paying commercials I had done years earlier. I asked if they had any work for me and was a little taken aback when they offered me a job working at the company as an assistant to the casting director. In other words, they offered me a desk job.

I took it, but I resented the job because I felt it was a step backward. But God knew what he was doing, even if I didn't. I had only seen casting through the eyes of a performer. Working on the other side gave me a unique perspective on the entire casting process. Years later, when I started my own company, I was able to put what I learned in this job to good use when I was casting my own films. But at the time, the whole thing seemed like a step back, if not an insult.

Working that desk job, I felt just like I had when I worked in the wheat field. This wasn't what I was meant to do! I began to dream of a way out. As desperate as I was, I still wasn't at the place where I was ready to ask God what he wanted for my life, but God was about to make his voice known.

SOMETHING BETTER FOR ME

One day in the summer of 1998, two actor friends, Brad Heller and Kevin Downes, and I were lamenting as to the sorry state of our careers and our limited prospects. We were willing to try anything different to get out of the rut we were stuck in. None of us had any experience in all of the many facets of film production. We didn't even have an idea of what story we wanted to tell. As actors, the only experience we had was showing up and having other people tell us what to do, what to say, and where to stand.

Back in my milk-and-honey days I had done a film with a man I called my godfather of Christian filmmaking, Rich Christiano. The four of us began talking about making Christian films, and Rich agreed to take us under his wing and mentor us in the business of film production.

It was an exciting and yet fretful time.

I slowly began to realize God had already provided what I needed by surrounding me with people who could teach me and who could help us produce our own films. He had reunited me with Rich Christiano at a time when I needed him to help me get started on producing a film. Other connections were a little more of a reach. The summer after my freshman year at Moody, when I'd worked on a film set at a camp in Wisconsin, I'd seen little value in that experience, and frankly I couldn't wait for it to end so I could get to Hollywood. However, the director of photography on that shoot was Wes Llewellyn. After Brad and Kevin and I decided to produce our own movie, I reached out to Wes and asked if he wanted to be involved in our venture. He and his wife began working on the screenplay for what would become the movie *The Moment After*. Things were falling into place.

Meanwhile Brad, Kevin, and I went to friends and family and raised $87,000 to produce the film. I say that now as though it was no big deal, but it was a *huge* deal. Who would have imagined that three out-of-work actors with no clue how to make a movie, let alone distribute it and make a profit, would be able to raise just under $100,000?

At the time, the Christian film business was in its infancy and at least twenty years behind the Christian music industry. I believed that one day, major studios would have Christian production divisions just like the major recording labels had, but for that to happen, the bar needed to be raised in terms of quality of production. If we were going to make a Christian film, I wanted to contemporize the genre and make a movie that people like my friends and I would want to see. In a word, I wanted the movie to be *cool*. There's a saying: Do what you know. Did I want to be a faith-based movie producer as a career? Not really; however, I didn't mind producing a faith-based movie.

The Moment After was like nothing the Christian community had ever seen. It appealed to younger audiences and was, for its time, considered a progressive film. The story featured two FBI agents (right out of the *X-Files*) who were sent to investigate mysterious disappearances as a result of the Rapture. The film not only delivered a strong Christian message, but it also included timely elements that appealed to mainstream audiences.

Our gamble paid off. *The Moment After* did very well and made back all of its money, in addition to a very healthy profit for its investors. We distributed the film to ministries and churches, opening up a new way for a film of this kind to achieve a profit.

MERCY STREETS

I had a strong feeling the Christian film market was set to explode much like the Christian music industry had done a couple decades before. With *The Moment After* under my belt, I wanted to further pave the way for excellence in Christian films and in doing so perhaps kick-start my failing mainstream acting career with our next project, a movie called *Mercy Streets*.

I had wanted to work with Jon Gunn, a good friend of mine who is both a very talented director and screenwriter. At the same time, businessman and entrepreneur Norm Miller, chairman of Interstate Batteries System of America, had recently started Providence Entertainment, the first Christian film distribution company in Hollywood specializing in faith-based movies. Providence had just released TBN's *The Omega Code*, the first feature-length Christian film to receive national theatrical release. Norm was a friend and mentor of mine, and he agreed to distribute my next film in theaters.

For the first time in years, doors were opening for me. The elements seemed to be converging in perfect alignment. When we set out to raise money for *Mercy Streets*, we managed to raise a million dollars, ten times what we had raised for *The Moment After*! And most importantly, *Mercy Streets* was going to be released and seen in movie theaters across the country.

In the film, I played the dual leading roles of twins who are separated at birth. One of the twins becomes a minister while the other turns to a life of crime and becomes a con artist. The irony of this scenario did not escape me. In his letter to the Romans, Paul writes, "I do not understand what I do. For what I want to do I do not do, but what I hate I do" (7:15). This was my life at the time. I was making films that promoted a Christian worldview, but I was still living a very un-Christian life. Embarrassed by my life, I found myself making excuses for it. I would say things like, "The girl I'm seeing isn't a believer, but she has a good heart," or "It's okay for me to hang out in the bar or that club because while temptation is all around me, I can handle it." I wasn't kidding anyone, least of all myself. The hypocrisy was starting to suffocate me.

I was trying to change, trying to go back to the person I once was by eliminating newly formed habits, choosing more carefully whom I befriended and dated, and trying to live the life I knew was right. However, I was so busy trying to get my life and career back on track that I had little time for Bible study and worship. To complicate matters, many of the people I was meeting weren't believers or had only a cursory relationship with God. I made too many excuses for my behavior and far too many compromises. I knew I had to get back on the right path, but soon I came to realize I could not do it alone. I could not find the strength within myself. Like Paul, I knew what was right, but I often did what I knew was wrong.

Mercy Streets opened to critical acclaim in theaters all around the world. The film was nominated for numerous awards, and I was nominated for a variety of acting awards. Suddenly it seemed as though mainstream Hollywood was interested in me again, and I took a slew of meetings with agents and casting directors, some of whom I had not seen in years. It was a high time for me. It looked as though after a long period of drought and famine I was finally going to be able to harvest the fruits of my labor, a cause for celebration.

After doing some quick math, I realize that this period in my life marks the halfway point between now and when I first moved to California about twenty years ago. Not incidentally, the midpoint or halfway mark of a movie is called the "The Point of No Return" or "False Victory/Defeat," where the hero crosses a threshold of some kind that leaves him no choice but to continue the journey. This shift into the second half of the story is usually characterized by a short-lived celebration or, alternatively, a period of mourning. It's a temporary situation because the victory or defeat the hero experiences at this juncture is merely transitional and not a genuine defeat or victory.

I point this out because art was about to imitate life.

A FALSE VICTORY

While I consider *Mercy Streets* to be one of my better films, it did nothing to promote or advance my career in mainstream Hollywood. All the attention and acclaim amounted to very little in the end. And worse, the movie was a financial bust. The film's financiers were at risk of losing their million-dollar investment.

It was as if the Lord had placed on me a cloak of some kind. All the meetings and praises didn't amount to anything. Once again, the doors to mainstream Hollywood were closing one by one, and this time it seemed as though they were being nailed shut. I still couldn't get arrested in this town. To quote the film *Jerry Maguire*, "Twenty-four hours ago, man, I was hot! Now . . . I'm a cautionary tale. You see this jacket I'm wearing, you like it? I don't really need it. Because I'm cloaked in failure!"

There are stories in the Bible where someone speaks with

God and comes away from that conversation with insight and direction. For instance, Moses encountered God, who spoke to him from a burning bush. After that conversation with God, Moses knew exactly what he was supposed to do, and his path was made very clear to him.

In real life, however, there is seldom a singularly isolated moment where everything suddenly makes sense and our paths are made clear to us. Likewise, I've never experienced a talking plant, on fire or otherwise. In my life, awareness was more of a process, a gradual evolution occurring over time. My conversations with God have not been characterized by a dove flying through a separation in the clouds, an angelic visitation, or fireballs. Like he did with Elijah before me, God spoke in a gentle whisper (1 Kings 19:1–18). His presence was revealed in the whispers of my childhood dream to become an actor and in his gentle nudging to stay near to him through both my failures and my victories. Amen.

After the disappointment of *Mercy Streets*, I asked for a sign from God. I so very much needed a burning bush moment to understand fully what he wanted from and for me. I was looking for that aha moment to put things in perspective and give me direction. After a time of prayer and reflection, I came to realize God had been speaking to me all along and that my life had already provided numerous moments I could have learned direction from. Looking back, I recognized dozens of little burning bushes along my journey. I didn't hear God because I was doing all of the talking and not enough listening. I didn't see the learning moments and signposts in my life because I was blinded by my own ambitions and self-serving interpretations of my God-given dream.

I took stock of my life. I considered the experiences that took place over the last ten years and laid them out end to end. The result was both shocking and enlightening. This condensed bird's-eye view revealed a conversation with God that had been happening in the background of my life, and I was in large part unaware of it.

MY BURNING BUSH

Allow me to recreate in a more conventional way the conversation I had been having over the past twenty years or so of my life. A conversation with God that started during my earliest years of recollection, when I was playing with *Star Wars* action figures or pretending I was a cowboy. The conversation continued throughout high school, during my year at Moody, and all the way to the present day. I'll take out all of the gaps in time, the misunderstandings, and my stubbornness and inability to hear God. For the sake of this illustration, imagine that I am asleep and God speaks to me in my dream.

"Psst. Hey, David," he would say.

"Lord? Is that you?"

"Yeah, I figured since you're sleeping you'd have some time for me. I'm sensing you're confused and frustrated."

"Yes. It's about my you-given dream. I figured since you gave the dream to me, things would work out if I lived a good Christian life."

"Hmm. Define 'work out.'"

"You know," I answer, kind of surprised I have to explain it. "That I would get everything I want."

"I see. Well . . ."

"I mean, I prayed and prayed about it. I've been talking to you

121

for years, and I feel like I'm not getting any answers. I remember this one time when I asked for the power of invisibility . . ."

"David . . ."

"Yes, Lord?"

"I love that you talk to me, but sometimes for *you* to get anything out of prayer, you have to leave some room for me to talk back."

"Oh, right. Sorry, Lord."

"Of course it pleases me when you're happy. That's part of the reason I instill a passion in people. It's so they will enjoy themselves while they're doing something for me."

"Sorry to interrupt again, but my dream of show business is for *you*?"

"Of course. I mean, we both get something out of it, but primarily I put the dream in your heart to serve my end."

"Wait a minute. How does my going to Hollywood, becoming a huge celebrity, making tons of cash, marrying a hot wife, driving a cool car, being adored by millions, and getting my name on the Hollywood Walk of Fame serve you?"

"Exactly."

"Oh."

"I put the dream of becoming an actor in your heart, but my vision for what that would look like is very different from yours. Your dream of being an actor is only a small part of my much bigger dream for you. You're unhappy now because you're trying to live your own dream instead of what I had planned for us."

"For us?"

"Yes, you and I. Don't you understand we're partners in the dream I put in your heart? We each have a role to play in it. And believe me, what I have in mind for us is so much better than a fast car or your name on a sidewalk."

"Well, what is it?"

"Wow. It only took you ten years to ask me. Look to the doors still open and stop trying to break down the ones I've already closed. Hand your depression and frustration over to me. Those emotions do you no good, and they're making such a racket you can't hear me over the noise."

"Open doors. Give my depression to you. Got it. I'm getting sleepy, Lord." I yawn.

"Goodnight, David."

I yawn again, my eyes suddenly so very heavy. "Lord . . . one more thing . . ."

"Yes, David?"

"About my hot wife . . ."

"Go to sleep, David."

Again, this conversation did not happen exactly this way, but you get the greater point. I finally understood that God was not interested in my success in mainstream Hollywood, and that he had other plans for me.

THE ROAD BACK HOME

My decision to leave the world of the con man and become a pastor (metaphorically speaking) was the real success of *Mercy Streets*. I made the decision to redevote my life to the Lord. I was tired of living the empty life of the unbeliever or the one who has fallen by the wayside. I want to make this very clear so I am not misunderstood. I was emotionally depleted not because of my inability to become a big Hollywood star but because I had been living a spiritually starved life. I no longer wanted to exist without purpose, direction, or reason. The rewards and accolades I was searching for were empty without God in my heart, guiding my steps. I missed my best friend, my Savior, and my heavenly Father.

I knew I had to work on removing sin from my life because it effectively put up a wall between God and me. It separated the two of us, making my situation worse because when I needed him most, I was pushing him away with my compromised life. I'm not going to lie; the journey back was at times difficult. I had developed some bad habits during my darker years, and a person doesn't change completely overnight, regardless of what the movies will tell you. But this time I had direction. I was headed back to the Lord to commit my life and my dreams to him. I was determined to continue to listen and discover what it was he wanted me to do with the rest of my life and allow him to use me for his glory. God had not abandoned or ignored me. Quite the contrary. I had wandered away from him, but he was always there, waiting for me to make even the smallest effort to hear him. I had wandered a thousand steps away from the Lord, but he was following me the whole time. All I needed to do was turn around and take one step back.

God is not in the career-building or dream-fulfilling business. God is in the kingdom-building business and wants to fulfill *his* dreams *for* you—not your dreams for yourself. He is most concerned with making and fostering disciples, not fabricating dreams.

"But wait a minute, you said at the beginning of this book . . ."

IT'S NOT ABOUT YOU

I know what I said. Hear me out. This is the rub. Not every dream you have is from God. Sometimes the dreams or goals you have are your own and not God's dream for you. Yes, God wants you to be happy, but the happiness God wants for you may not be what you've pictured for yourself.

When I left Kansas, my dream was all about *me*. Yes, my dream to act, to go into the entertainment industry was from God, but I failed to grasp *why* he had given me that dream. Instead, I focused on myself. I wanted to get this and I wanted to achieve that. As it turned out, the Lord wasn't really having much of that. I'll go so far as to suggest God didn't really care about my dreams, not as long as the word *my* was so firmly imbedded in them. To get the support I so desperately needed from God, I had to first start dropping all of the *me's* and the *my's* out of the conversation.

Many of us are familiar with the verse, "'For I know the plans I have for you,' declares the LORD, 'plans to prosper you and not to harm you, plans to give you hope and a future'" (Jeremiah 29:11). While I do believe God has placed a dream in your heart and that he has a purpose and plan for you, the process begins with you first abandoning "you." This shouldn't come as a surprise. As Jesus plainly told his followers: "Whoever wants to be my disciple must deny themselves and take up their cross daily and follow me" (Luke 9:23).

Unless your dream is a God-given dream, its fulfillment will be problematic. Even if you "succeed," your victory will ultimately be unsatisfying and shallow without God at its center. Take comfort and strength knowing God's dream for our lives is better than our own.

Jesus told his disciples that without him, our efforts are in vain and all of our dreams will be frustrated. Jesus was very clear about this when he said he was the vine and we are all as branches connected to him. No branch can live, let alone produce fruit, by itself. Further, Jesus underscored the point by saying, "Apart from me you can do nothing" (John 15:5). The source of life and spiritual fruit cannot be found or harvested within ourselves; it exists outside of us, solely within Christ Jesus. The strength, nourishment, and creativity needed to fulfill our dreams must come from Jesus. I had spent most of my professional life trying to go at it alone and with my own strength.

DETERMINING WHICH OF YOUR DREAMS IS FROM GOD

So the million-dollar question is, how do you determine which of your dreams is from God? Why waste your time and effort trying to achieve something doomed from the start? Take a long, honest look at the dreams in your heart. Be truthful with yourself as you put your dreams through the following paces. Ask yourself:

Is Your Dream Bigger Than You?

Children dream fantastic dreams of becoming astronauts, major league football players, or rock-and-roll stars. As they grow older, those grand dreams become little more than fantasies. Circumstances and real-world limitations shave those dreams down to a realistic and manageable size. In many cases, we adults do this to ourselves of our own volition, so as not to be disappointed or look silly.

And this is exactly the opposite of what we should be doing. As we get older, our dreams should keep pace, and we should be setting higher goals for ourselves, not minimizing them. Your dreams should grow to be so big there would be no realistic way for you to achieve them. Unless . . .

You turn to God for his guidance and strength. If you think you can go it alone, then you're not dreaming big enough.

A dream that is connected to God's purposes will be bigger than your resources, talents, connections, and abilities. It will tower over you and cause you to become weak in the knees. If you think your dream is impossible to achieve, then that's a good sign you're probably on the right track. For instance, maybe you have a dream of studying carpentry so one day you can save a few dollars and build your own entertainment center or put up some shelves. There is nothing wrong with that, and I hope the shelves come out okay, but it's not the kind of dream I am talking about in this book. Now, if you tell me you spend your days in an office selling insurance but have this persistent and nagging desire to learn about construction and architecture so you can design, manufacture, and build low-cost housing for the poor and the homeless, I would say that's a God-sized dream, and you're going to need a lot of help from him.

When we talk about big dreams, or dreams that are bigger than us, oftentimes grand and amazing images of success and groundbreaking innovation come to mind. And that's fine.

But a dream that is bigger than you doesn't have to involve world records, groundbreaking technology, or large sums of money in order to be God given and impossible without his help. Here's a case in point.

I met a woman at a conference where I was speaking who told me she had no elevated or fantastic dreams. She said she simply wanted a loving marriage with her husband and to raise her children in the way of the Lord. Oh my. You want to talk about impossible without the Lord? Marriage and family are institutions that God needs to be invited into if you hope to have any success. In Matthew 7:24–27, Jesus warns us about the storms of life. He is telling us that floods, wind, and the like will assault our marriages, and unless we are spiritually prepared, these elements are bound to wreak havoc in our home lives. Family is fundamentally important to God and his purposes, and the goal to do it right is a God-sized dream, to be sure, so you will need his help to achieve it.

So ask yourself, Does the enormity of my dream scare me? Does the impossibility of my dream cause me to cry out for God's direction, strength, and wisdom? Is my dream *only* possible by faith? If it is, then keep reading.

Does Your Dream Have a Hold on You?

Remember what happened in the Dr. Seuss book *The Cat in the Hat Comes Back?* The Cat in the Hat eats a cake in the tub and leaves a pink ring around it. Each attempt at wiping the spot clean from the bathtub proves unsuccessful as the pink mess is only transferred to another item in the house. I remember wondering what that pink mess was. I thought it had to be the stickiest stuff in the universe.

Here's the thing. If your dream is truly from God, then it will feel much the same way. Just like the pink goo from the children's classic, the more you try to wipe it off of you, the more it will spread. A God-given dream is a persistent and clinging thing that will not be wiped from your heart.

There may be seasons in your life when the dream is less bothersome and doesn't appear to be picking at the edges of your heart. You might even go quite awhile without thinking about it, but eventually it will once again rise to the surface, tap you on the shoulder, and demand your attention.

This is not to say you will never have other ideas or other goals, but like anything else, they will tend to evaporate over time. Is there one dream, however, that lingers? Does one dream refuse to leave you? If so, then maybe God is trying to tell you something.

Will You Pay the Price for Your Dream?

When I ask if you are willing to "pay the price," I'm asking if you are willing to invest all of your time and energy into your dream. Think of your dream as a newborn baby, because it's going to need the same level of dedication and commitment for it to grow and be fulfilled. Does your dream inspire in you that kind of devotion, the kind you'd give your own child? It will need to, and if it does, then it might be God whispering to you.

Will Your Dream Outlive You?

Billionaire banker Uday Kotak once said, "If what you create does not outlive you, then you have failed."

Our celebrity-obsessed culture glorifies the most fleeting and temporary of accomplishments. We celebrate and honor record-breaking sales, fame, wealth, and power, but these things never last. Today's top scores, box office bonanzas, and record sales will one day be bested and then forgotten. Today's world no longer offers fifteen minutes of fame. These days you can go from hero to zero in about ninety seconds.

If the fruits of your dreams will fade and lose impact over time, then you've built them on the wrong foundation. Ego, pride, fame, money, and tradition are all flimsy foundations that can't support your dream. Don't tell me your dream is to produce the largest-selling CD of all time or top the world record for the fifty-yard dash and then walk away, thinking you can't fail because God put that dream into your heart. Instead, remember, "All people are like grass, and all their glory is like the flowers of the field; the grass withers and the flowers fall, but the word of the Lord endures forever" (1 Peter 1:24–25).

The Bible tells us there are a few things that last forever: faith, hope, love, and the Word of God. God is not interested in fads and fashions. If your dream is a God-given one, it will be supported by and built upon God's never-changing foundation of truth and love.

Does Your Dream Glorify God?

Everything God made, he did so for his glory. The apostle Paul could not be any more clear: "For from him and through him and for him are all things. To him be the glory forever! Amen" (Romans 11:36).

To glorify God is to praise and exalt his attributes, including his mercy, grace, love, and omniscience, to name just a few. It means to honor him with our behavior, how we act and think. We glorify God with our faith, trust, and obedience. To glorify God is to submit to him in all our ways and to acknowledge his glory, valuing it above all things.

Not incidentally, we also glorify God by making him known to others by what is called "rehearsing his deeds and attributes." Essentially, when we tell people of God's work or who he is, we glorify him before others. Hold onto this thought because later I'm going to bring it up again.

Be particularly honest with yourself when you put your dream to the "Glory of God" test. Don't sugarcoat or gloss over the reality. Don't waste your time or your life chasing after a dream built on a crumbling foundation. Your dream cannot reflect poorly on God or his Word. I'm not saying you have to drape Christian fish stickers on everything you do, but a dream that hovers in a "gray area" of morality or tries to find loopholes in his commandments does not glorify the Lord.

Does Your Dream Serve Others?

Finally, does your dream encourage you to help others in some way? To solve problems and meet the needs of others? If your dream is only self-serving, then it's not the big dream God has in mind for you. Remember that God conceived and intended for us to serve others. The apostle Peter wrote, "Each of you should use whatever gift you have received to serve others, as faithful stewards of God's grace in its various forms" (1 Peter 4:10).

I'm not saying you won't benefit from your dream. You most certainly will, but it may cost you dearly.

Will your dream soothe human suffering in some way, fill a need, or solve a problem, or does it simply get your picture in the newspaper? If God given, your dream will give without expecting anything in return. Motivational speaker Leo Buscaglia once said, "Your talent is God's gift to you. What you do with it is your gift back to God."

I don't want to harp on this. I know some of you are thinking right now, "Yeah, yeah. We get it. Do for others. Our God-given dreams are service oriented in nature." But here is why it is important. Many dreams are "me" centered. "I'm going to do this," we say, and "I'm going to do that, and the sense of achievement I get from accomplishing my dreams is going to make me feel complete." I know how you feel because that is exactly how I felt. Please hear me out, because chances are God is not having it.

Christians are here to make a difference, not only in our own lives but also *in the world*. Jesus Christ came to earth so that we could make a difference in *other people's lives*. Jesus's own disciples asked him what the greatest commandment was. He answered that we should love God and love other people, declaring that "all the Law and the Prophets hang on these two commandments" (Matthew 22:40). It's so important that you understand this simple yet profound concept.

Does your dream speak to the love of God and other people? Does it fulfill what Jesus called the greatest commandments? Maybe I'm so passionate about this point because during my first years in Los Angeles, my dream did not.

And that's why I had to let it go.

To see photos of David on sets in the early 2000s and from the set of one of his favorite films, Mercy Streets, visit DavidARWhite.com /Exclusive.

CHAPTER 7

When Plan "A" Doesn't Work, Remember God Has Twenty-Five More Letters

*A bend in the road is not the end of the
road, unless you fail to make the turn.*

Helen Keller

I n the movie *Rocky*, the title character wants nothing more than to perform respectfully against the heavyweight champion of the world, but he is defeated in the title fight. Rocky is still victorious, however, because although he loses the decision against the reigning champ, he has won the heart of his true love, Adrian.

I had touched bottom and was armed with a new resolve. And it was at this juncture that I was about to meet my "Adrian."

TRYING HARD NOW

In 1998, Brad Heller and I had managed to scrape just enough money together to put it down on a small duplex situated in the Hollywood Hills. Brad lived upstairs while I occupied the house's bottom story. This arrangement was about to come in handy.

Mercy Streets had lost money, so I was broke again, but with the extra space I had in the duplex, I was able to take a roommate to help with expenses. I wasn't happy about the movie losing money, but I was determined not to let it blow me off course. I had made a decision to grow closer to the Lord, and I wasn't going to let any setbacks, financial or otherwise, get in my way.

I formed a Bible study group based on the *Navigator 2:7 Series*, the same program my father had used to disciple me when I was young. I started the group with my new roommate and soon was joined by half a dozen actors and musicians, all of whom were hungry for the Word. It was not the most comfortable thing I've ever done, and men can be reluctant to share their feelings and thoughts, but I soon grew accustomed to "feeling comfortable in the uncomfortable." We were just a collection of broken guys, all drawn to the town that promises everything but doesn't offer the Truth. We knew we needed a Savior.

I spent the next year learning how to edit movie trailers at a company with my friend Jon Gunn. Trailers are those little two-minute shorts that advertise a movie that's coming soon. They play at the theater before the main feature. I am not technically inclined, but it was a job, and I needed the money to survive and to pay my share of the mortgage on the duplex. The low-stress and low-responsibility position gave me time to sit with myself and with God in relative calm and quiet. And once again I was learning an invaluable aspect of movie making that would come in handy down the road. I had faith that when the Lord was ready for me to hear my new direction, then he would make it known to me. Until then, there was something else I think he wanted me to concentrate on first. Or should I say, *someone* else.

I met her in church—a beautiful young woman in her early twenties, sporting the longest set of dreadlocks I had ever seen on a white woman. I later learned her name was Andrea, but at that moment she looked more like Bo Derek from the movie *10*. I would also learn to find her devotion to the Lord and passion for Jesus to be her most attractive feature. My parents had advised me to marry a woman who was devoted to Christ, and while I had certainly dated many who were not, I think on some level I was waiting for this very moment and this very woman.

I was determined to court Andrea in the proper way. I was careful not to let some of my old habits poison or pollute my relationship with her. We went out on group dates at first because she was very guarded, and it was the only way for me to get to know her.

But then she kept disappearing on me. I would see her come in late to the first church service and afterwards try to have a conversation with her, but I wouldn't be able to find her. Other times I didn't even have the good fortune to spot her in church, much less have a conversation with her. Then I switched churches around that time, and it would be a year before I would see her again. I learned later Andrea had just come to the Lord, and I believe that he wanted Andrea to himself, to give her the chance to grow in him. For my part, I needed the time to mature and shed some of my newly acquired worldly ways. I was frustrated by Andrea's departure, but I was coming to a place where I trusted that God knew what he was doing, so I accepted it and continued to work on myself.

I spent this next year in Bible study and fellowship, and I

attended this great church called The Malibu Vineyard, where I discovered so many folks like myself. A ton of industry people, some famous, others not so much, who put all of the glitz and glamor aside to worship the Lord and share in his grace. The worship music was awesome, as many in the choir and band were Grammy Award nominees and winners.

Then one day I ran into Andrea coming out of a Bible study that I attended for years but had not been to for a while. It was called Media Fellowship and was for actors in the industry. I was more than stunned. I think I managed to mumble, "What are you doing here?" or something equally as suave. Somewhere in our nervous banter, Andrea said she was working with Ewan McGregor on a new movie, and the assistant director had invited her. Then the most unexpected thing came out of her mouth: "I think I'm ready for my husband." We were both taken aback that she said such a thing, but even so, it seemed the perfect thing for her to say. We went hiking together soon after. I showed up in high tops and breakaway sweats, but somehow Andrea overlooked it, and I never let her out of my sight again. We were married a year later.

GETTING STRONG NOW

In 2002 I began to feel centered again. I was no longer interested in pursuing a career whose grand design was only to elevate and exalt myself. I knew God had given me the dream to become an actor so that, ultimately, I could impact others for him. My spiritual reawakening and my relationship with Andrea gave me the courage to get back in the saddle. This time, however, the "saddle" was a bit different than those I had ridden in before.

My producing partner at the time, Kevin Downes, and I wanted to make an end times movie called *Six: The Mark*

Unleashed, but we knew raising the money would be difficult since *Mercy Streets* had underperformed. I was not deterred. I felt in my heart this was the path God wanted me to take, and I left the issue of financing in his hands.

Our prayers began to be answered not so much by dollars but by some fortunate casting opportunities. The first was that actor Jeffrey Dean Morgan agreed to star in *Six: The Mark Unleashed*. Just after starring in our movie, he would simultaneously appear in three separate television series: *Supernatural*, *Weeds,* and *Grey's Anatomy*, where he made his mark.

Then I got a phone call from Stephen Baldwin, who was on set in Romania shooting his new movie. He had recently announced his conversion to Christianity, and he called to express an interest in doing a film for the faith market. Stephen had read the script for *Six: The Mark Unleashed* and wanted to play the role of the angel. I felt the inclusion of these two fine actors was a sign that we were on the right track.

Production came to a halt when our tiny budget of $150,000 ran out, and we found ourselves over budget and without any money to finish the film. The Trinity Broadcasting Network became a partner and pulled us out of the fire by investing another $750,000 into the project. Prayer after prayer was being answered. *Six: The Mark Unleashed* went on to perform very well, selling over 400,000 DVD units.

Kevin and I were on a winning streak and immediately went into production of *The Moment After 2*. All of this happened during the real estate boom in California during the mid-2000s. I sold my share of the duplex back to Brad and made quite a bit of profit on the deal. I was able to buy a house in Eagle Rock, California, that was better suited for Andrea and me to raise a family in. Things were turning around. Doors that had previously been closed to me were opening up.

That's not to say that these times were easy. We were pioneering a completely new genre in American filmmaking. There were no rules or precedent to speak of, and many of our efforts were akin to guerrilla marketing. It was exciting but also very demanding.

It was during this time of successful movie making and fast-paced real estate deals that Kevin told me he felt called to stop making smaller, independent films and instead go the studio route. I couldn't blame him. Our road was a tremendous amount of work with little financial reward.

But I had a clear understanding of why God had given me my dream, and I didn't feel I could fulfill it if I became a "producer for hire." I wanted to make movies that brought the Christian worldview to the forefront, and I wanted to make them on a consistent basis. I felt that was the direction God was pointing me in. It wasn't that I had a problem with mainstream movie making or that I was opposed to it based on some moral principle; it was more the Lord had shut those doors and left open others.

WORKING HARD NOW

I had helped Andrea get a job working with Michael Scott, a friend who made commercials for BMW automobiles. He also ran a postproduction house and had helped us out on some of our films. During this time, Andrea kept encouraging me to partner with Mike because she felt the two of us had similar sensibilities and a love for the Lord. Mike had been watching Kevin's and my success over the last few years, as he had always wanted to enter the world of commercial filmmaking.

Mike and I became business partners, and it wasn't long before he introduced me to Russell Wolfe, a brilliant promoter who agreed to be another partner. Russ didn't know much about movie making, but he had a great mind for business and a passion to do something with eternal value.

The year was 2005, and the three of us formed a company called Pure Flix, an independent production and distribution entity whose mission is to influence the global culture for Christ through media. This wasn't what I had thought I would be doing, but it was exactly what I was supposed to be doing. Life isn't always about finding yourself. More often than not, it's about discovering who God created you to be.

A PAT ON THE BACK

Our first film as a newly formed company, *Hidden Secrets*, was one that explored the hurts and mistakes we often hide from our friends, family, and fellow churchgoers. My parents were proud of the film and what our company was doing. I arranged for both my mom and dad to appear in the film. My father pats me on the back in a scene where I enter a church.

About a week before *Hidden Secrets* had a two-night showing at a Fathom Event, my father called and said, "David, you're really good at this acting and producing thing. I want you to do more of it, and it will be amazing to see where God takes you with it. I'm proud of you, son." The next morning he entered the hospital for a routine hernia operation. He came home later that day to take a nap and never woke up from it.

I guess his body was just exhausted. Like many saints in the Bible, my father toiled endlessly, never to truly see the fruit of his labor. Yet his memorial was packed with person after person who stood up and gave testimony on how my father had impacted their lives.

That night, after my father's funeral, I went to the premiere of *Hidden Secrets* and watched the scene where my father patted me on the back. I remembered his last words to me, "I'm proud of you." In a curious turn of events, I was now living my father's dream for me—it just looked a bit different than what he or I had imagined. I was in ministry, married to a woman who loved the Lord, and serving Christ in whatever I did. I had to give up my small dream in order to adopt God's grand dream for me.

I've prayed for many things in my life, but of all the times I've prayed and all the many things I've prayed for, it wasn't until that day in Los Angeles when things seemed so bleak for me that I prayed for God to open the doors he wanted open and to close those he didn't. It was a variation of the "Show me the way, Lord" prayer, but this time I was being more specific. I was asking God to make his will clear by removing all other options and distractions. I was asking for roadblocks and dead ends. I knew I needed impenetrable obstacles to stop me from continuing down the wrong path. I prayed for him to close the doors and allow me to see them shut.

Sometimes we have to have our dreams stalled or denied so we can get on the right path. We have to hear the word *no* in order to get to where God wants us to be. There are occasions when in order to experience the best version of what God has planned for us, we have to abandon our own vision and ideas of what that is.

Following Jesus requires not only a surrender of the self, but along with that, a willingness to accept wholeheartedly his will for you, whatever that may look like.

You have to remain open to the possibility that your dream may have to die in order for you to unearth and recognize God's new and improved version of your dream. As you've seen, God closed doors for me until I was spiritually on track and ready to give him glory rather than seeking glory for myself. But sometimes God closes doors so that we can't fulfill a dream because he has a new dream for us. Galatians 6:9 tells us, "Let us not become weary in doing good, for at the proper time we will reap a harvest if we do not give up."

But what about when your dream isn't about doing good or when, upon closer examination, you discover your dream is no longer making good sense? No one expects you to waste your life running down the wrong path, no matter how good it looks on a bumper sticker.

If you are currently in the middle of a longtime pursuit of your dream with little to show for it, then you owe it to yourself and to God to take a step back and reevaluate. If you feel as though God has closed the door on your dream, then maybe he has.

WHEN IT'S TIME TO LET GO: GOD IS SAYING NO

We know that in order to live a truly enriched life, we must ask God to direct our path. There are times when we must be willing to abandon our dreams in order that we can continue on with our lives and make room for God's new dreams for us. We all may come to a point in our journeys when we have to let go of what was and have faith in what will be.

How does one determine when it is time to let go of a dream? This is a very personal question, and I don't have a clear-cut, definitive answer for you. I can only advise you to get alone with God and work through this. Pray with like-minded friends and mentors mature in their spiritual walk.

There is no one-size-fits-all solution here. I can only offer guidelines and warning signs from my own experience. In my case, God was closing doors in order to effect change in my heart before he changed the situation and circumstances around me. Philippians 1:6 says, in effect, "Be patient. God isn't finished with you yet." In other cases, closed doors simply mean a dream needs to be set on the back burner temporarily. I've heard it said that God answers our prayers in one of three ways: yes, no, or wait. A dream deferred is not always a dream denied. "Not now" doesn't always mean "No."

But if you have sought God's guidance and the counsel of wise and godly friends, and you feel that he wants you to give up your dream, then you need to pay attention and let go. Perhaps it was never a God-given dream in the first place and served only your ego. Or perhaps God has something new in store for you. You may find something nagging at you from the fringes of your conscience, or perhaps over time your dream has slowly become a source of anxiety for you, no longer leaving you with positive feelings. If so, surrender your frustrated and failed dreams to God.

WHEN IT'S TIME TO CHANGE YOUR APPROACH
The Pursuit of My Dream Is Hurting Me

Have you lost yourself in the pursuit of your dream? Have you drained your bank account and jeopardized your financial future? Has it caused your health to fail? Have you sacrificed so much of who you once were that your relationship with God is suffering?

Of course there must be sacrifices along the way. Any God-given dream will be worth the price there is to pay. But if you are causing irreparable damage to your personhood, finances, health, or spiritual well-being, then maybe it's time to let go and trust God with the outcome.

The Pursuit of My Dream Is Hurting Others

A friend of mine is a struggling screenplay writer. He has a wife and two children. He met with a good degree of success during his first years in Los Angeles, but about ten years ago things soured for him and he fell on cripplingly hard financial times. After exhausting his friends and family's resources to the tune of tens of thousands of dollars, he was evicted from his home in the dead of night and forced to pack his family up and move to another state, where for six months he, his wife, and their two children lived in a tiny guest bedroom. His children missed a year of school and were both held back. His wife could not take the strain and fear of not knowing what the next day would bring and eventually left him for another man.

All along I kept asking my friend why he let things get so out of hand. Why hadn't he put his writing career on hold and looked for another job to pay the bills? His answer was always the same. He felt as though he'd be giving up on his dream of being a successful screenwriter. He didn't want his wife and children to see him as a "quitter." Not only was his stubborn dedication to his dream selfish, it was also irresponsible and damaging to his family.

143

When your dream is destroying your relationships or your family, something needs to change, and it may very well be your dream. Don't kid yourself into thinking that one day you will make it big and the financial boon will make up for the sacrifice. No amount of money is worth losing or harming your family over. We can never evaluate the success of an endeavor solely on how much money it makes us. Remember: "What good is it for someone to gain the whole world, yet forfeit their soul?" (Mark 8:36).

My Dream Has Become an Idol

Remember that line from the film *Jerry Maguire* where Tom Cruise tells Renee Zellweger, "You complete me." Has your dream become your one true love? Are you depending on the dream to complete you or to satisfy and fulfill you entirely? Are you looking for your dream to give you definitive purpose and an identity? If so, then your dream that was meant to be a form of worship to God has in fact *become* your god. But the dream is never the destination. Christ himself is always the endgame.

Be careful not to worship your dream. Worship only God, or your dream will jeopardize your relationships and fail to meet the needs that only God can. God will not give you what you want until you want it for the right reasons.

I know you have probably spent much of your life thinking the fulfillment of your dreams will satisfy all the desires of your heart. It's why you pray for clarity. It's why you've spent so much time fantasizing about your dream or planning and plotting to achieve it. It's probably why you bought this book. But I'd like to redirect your thinking if I can.

We all must have faith that God is fully aware of our hearts' longings. Just as important, however, is the realization that God wants to be the fulfillment of those desires *himself*. He doesn't want us looking to our dreams to complete us, to give us wholeness, direction, purpose, or salvation. He wants us to look to him for those things.

A CAUTIONARY TALE

While researching this book, I came across a study spanning over four decades that examined the common regrets of the dying. Their number one regret is for the things they never did, the loss of their unfulfilled dreams.

Closer inspection, however, revealed a cautionary tale. What of those who did pursue their dreams? What of those who had achieved their loftiest goals? What were the most common regrets of the rich, the famous, the accomplished, and the most celebrated? The answers are sobering:

- They wish they'd heeded the warning signs and reevaluated their goals and dreams before sacrificing so much. Many of them felt they had never really lived and were unclear on who they were or what they wanted out of life. *God Is Saying No*
- They wish they had not worked so hard and ignored their health while they still had the chance to do something about it. *The Pursuit of My Dream Is Hurting Me*
- They regret pursuing money at the expense of relationships. *The Pursuit of My Dream Is Hurting Others*
- They regret allowing their goals and accomplishments to define them and therefore limit them. *My Dream Has Become an Idol*

When I told you earlier not to give up on your dreams, I didn't mean for you to keep banging your head against the wall with little or no appreciable results. Perhaps God wants you to let go of your dream so that he can replace it with a new dream. Or perhaps it's not your dream that needs to change but your methods. Maybe the ways in which you are going about achieving it are in need of an overhaul. Maybe it's time to redirect your thinking and to visualize your dream differently. Stay flexible and less rigid in the pursuit of your dreams, and by doing so you might discover a superior dream—one that is easier for you to accomplish and infinitely more gratifying both in this world and in the next.

Too many people believe that faith is defined by a belief that God will make our dreams and goals happen if we simply entrust them to him. I know because I was one of these people.

Instead, faith is a firm trust and conviction that sometimes if God doesn't give you what you think you want, it's not because you don't deserve it, but because you deserve better.

Check out never-before-seen photos of personal moments from David and Andrea's wedding day, as well as photos of David hanging out with Chuck Norris on the set of Bells of Innocence *at DavidARWhite .com/Exclusive.*

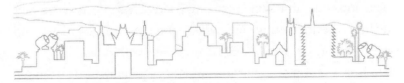

CHAPTER 8

Don't Hate the Wait

*Have courage for the great sorrows of life and
patience for the small ones; and when you
have laboriously accomplished your daily
task, go to sleep in peace. God is awake.*

Victor Hugo

There are many facets to filmmaking, but production and distribution are two of the most elementary. Most people understand the notion of film production. It's the "Lights. Camera. Action!" of it all. The media and the award events celebrate everything from the actors and music to the costumes and the editing. If film production is the star, then film distribution is the "weird uncle" of the film industry family.

Distribution is simply the process of making a movie available for people to watch it. I say "simply," but the task is far from simple. While it's not nearly as sexy as film production, distribution is arguably more important than its glamorous relative. Virtually anyone, and I mean *anyone*, can make a movie. If you go outside with your cell phone and shoot your kids giving your dog a bath, then you've a made a movie. The much harder task is figuring out a way to let people know you've made this movie, making it available for them to watch, and getting them to pay for the privilege of doing so. That's where a distribution company comes in. They generally make all of the decisions affecting your film after it is completed. These decisions might include the marketing and advertising, the release date, and what platform or media will be used for exhibition.

It can cost a tremendous amount of money to distribute a film, and the rewards can be considerably high. Bottom line: Film distribution can be an extremely lucrative field but comes at sizeable risk.

When Pure Flix finished the production of *Hidden Secrets*, we handed the film over to Genius Products, a distribution company that had recently merged with The Weinstein Company. All we could do at this point was wait, as the future of *Hidden Secrets* was beyond our control. Mike, Russ, and I took this time to plan Pure Flix's next and second venture, a little film called *The Wager*.

MOVING FORWARD

I had met country and western star Randy Travis on the set of *The Visitation*, a film based on the popular Frank Peretti novel of the same name and produced by my former partner Kevin Downes for Twentieth Century Fox. I had enjoyed working with Randy and thought he'd be perfect for the lead role in *The Wager*. It took some time, but after some Herculean efforts we managed to convince him to take a chance on our small upstart company, and he agreed to appear in the film.

Working with Randy gave us the opportunity to meet and develop a working relationship with Randy's then wife and long-time manager, Elizabeth Travis, or Liz, as she has been called for years. Liz discovered Randy when he was only nineteen years old while working in a nightclub she managed. In addition to having an eye for talent, Liz is a brilliant businessperson and loved the idea of using films for ministry. My partners and I were interested in approaching Liz to invest in our company, but to do that we had to get by her business manager, Gary Haber.

Gary had been in the business for a long time, and his clients included the likes of Peter Frampton, Lynyrd Skynyrd, and Michael Jackson, among other notables. Nervous about speaking with him because we had only $13.67 in our bank account, we were in definite need of more capital. We stayed up all night preparing our numbers and perfecting our presentation in an effort to convince him to convince Liz that investing in our company was a sound financial idea. After our song and dance, Gary told us, "Guys, I really like you, but in no way will I ever endorse investing in your movie company to my client."

My partners and I left Gary's office crestfallen. We went to lunch and ordered water with a basket of chips and salsa. It was all our company could afford! We all were wondering, "Lord, how are you going to make this work?" Had Pure Flix already met its end? Had the Lord only wanted us to form the company so that we could produce one film? Did he now have another plan for us? We were willing to do whatever it was that God wanted us to do. I, for one, was done trying to swim upstream against his desires for me, so I prayed for direction.

His direction came a short time later when we learned that Elizabeth Travis had ignored her business manager's advice and decided to invest in Pure Flix. We were able to finish our production of *The Wager,* all the while thinking, *We're on fire now. Everything is going to rocket to the top!*

SETBACK

In the movie *Rocky Balboa*, Rocky says, "It ain't about how hard you hit. It's about how hard you can get hit and keep moving forward." We were about to get hit.

We entrusted the distribution of both of our films to Genius Products for several reasons. Their distribution arms went much deeper into the market than ours did. We were new to this side of the business and thought our investors would be better serviced with a more experienced entity. At the time, production seemed all we could handle, and even though it had been our original plan to take our movies from A to Z, at the last minute we decided we just didn't have the large amounts of cash needed to do a proper job. Our initial plan seemed too big, so instead of trusting the Giver of dreams, we handed over the distribution rights to another company.

Both *Hidden Secrets* and *The Wager* performed well, and we are proud of them. But we encountered a major setback when, after collecting all of the money generated by those films, Genius Products went out of business, declaring bankruptcy. It was a difficult experience for us and for our investors, but we learned from it and vowed to never again make the mistake of entrusting our film distribution to another company.

BOUNCE BACK

There was simply no time for tears and regrets. Andrea and I now had a son, Ethan, our first child. I had a family to provide for and a company to run and keep afloat. I believe that God wants his children to keep moving even if we are waiting for him to show us what he wants us to do next (it's called active waiting!). So that's what we decided to do.

Mike left for Thailand and stayed six months shooting a couple of movies for us while Russ and I stayed behind to hold the fort. Then Russ called me one day and told me he knew a guy who knew a guy in Mexico who wanted to do a movie on his 120-foot yacht. He didn't care if it was a Christian movie or a Western; he just wanted to shoot a movie on his yacht. What do you say to that except, "Okay."

We developed the movie *In the Blink of an Eye* to be shot almost entirely on the yacht. We set our budget under $200,000, making it considerably easier for the film to return a profit for its investors and to keep Pure Flix afloat for another day.

We planned as best we could. Russ secured hotels in Mexico for the cast and crew to stay in and even managed to get us free meals. Of course the meals consisted entirely of burritos, three times a day, but they were free. Everything was in order. Our i's were dotted and our t's were crossed. There are, however, some things you just cannot plan for.

We were shooting on an island in the Sea of Cortez when we discovered that Mr. Yacht Owner had not paid his taxes to the Mexican government, and the government had sent the navy to commandeer his yacht. Not only was the yacht our principal set for production, but it was also our only mode of transportation off the island.

Russ said he'd handle it because that is what Russ does. He handles things. The rest of us went back to work and shot all day on the beach until the sun started to set and we realized we had eaten all of our burritos. Mild anxiety began to turn into abject freak-out when we realized our cell phones had zero reception, and no one had heard from or seen Russ in over twelve hours. Imagine a film crew of about twenty people stranded on a beach in a foreign country with no food, water, cell phone reception, or transportation out. Our faith was the only thing we had going for us at that moment, so we did what Christians do, and we began to pray for God to deliver us out of this sticky situation.

As night fell and we were cloaked in darkness, our script supervisor, a very vocal nonbeliever on the set, began to panic. Now I had another problem on my hands. While it certainly wasn't my fault that Mr. Yacht Owner owed the Mexican government back taxes, I did feel responsible for the safety and well-being of all the cast and crew stuck on the beach. Should we wait it out and perhaps spend the night on the beach, or should we try to gather everything, crew and equipment, and attempt a hike toward somewhere that resembled civilization? We were split as to what to do.

The script supervisor got more and more panicked as time went by with no help in sight. "Why pray?" she yelled. "Russ is not coming back, and God is certainly not going to help!" Just at that moment, the cavalry appeared over the horizon in the form of several huge 4x4 trucks. Russ had spent the day haggling with the Mexican government and somehow had managed to plead our case and now had come to rescue us off the island. I'm still not sure how he found us, but then again, it was just another day in the life of an independent film producer and a lesson to have patience and wait for things to unfold in God's time.

POP GOES THE BUBBLE

The year 2008 was the beginning of a long struggle for my family and for Pure Flix. The economic crisis that hit our country due to the real estate bubble made our financial situation challenging once again.

Earlier I had refinanced my home in Eagle Rock in order to survive as Pure Flix struggled to establish a foothold in the Christian faith-based film market. The house had almost doubled in value in just a few short years, and I was using the equity to pay the bills. Additionally, Mike Scott and I had purchased investment property in Florida a couple of years earlier. When the real estate bubble popped, I found myself upside down in all of these properties. Like millions of Americans, I was forced to short-sell my home and investment properties. Andrea and I lost just about everything we had put together over the last five years. We packed up our remaining possessions and moved into an apartment. It was a frightening time for all of us, and we were unsure of the road ahead.

I had faced times like this before, but in many ways this stress and pressure was worse. In the past, I had only myself to think of. This time I had a family to consider.

While I was concerned for the financial health and future of my family, I didn't crumble like I had in the past. In many ways I was better prepared for what was happening because I had learned some things about myself and God's will.

I had learned that as a child of God, I was not exempt from trial and adversity. I had learned to entrust myself to God during these hard years. I had a vision now, a vision I shared with God. Yes, the issues of the day were worrisome and often inconvenient, but I did my best to count my blessings and keep my eye on the long term. I knew what God wanted me to do, and since Pure Flix was truly a God-given dream, I knew that ultimately the company would not fail. That is not to say we wouldn't continue to experience ups and downs, wins and losses, breakthroughs and setbacks. This is the cyclic nature of life. Losing is a part of winning. I knew we had to be patient and wait for God to act in his time.

I was unable to draw a salary from Pure Flix for the next two years, so I survived by teaching acting classes in San Diego. The irony did not escape me that in order to make a living, I had returned to the town I started in when I first moved to California. I had taken acting classes when I moved to San Diego, and now I was returning there to teach them.

God tells us, "But as for you, be strong and do not give up, for your work will be rewarded" (2 Chronicles 15:7). This verse described our motto for Pure Flix for the next few years. While any company needs cash flow in order to keep the doors open, my partners and I weren't looking for only a financial reward. We needed to stay afloat in order to give our fledgling company a chance to make a difference in people's spiritual lives. The company managed to persevere despite a downward turn in the economy and our near-crippling experience with the distribution company that went bankrupt. Somehow we kept going in the face of mounting impossibilities associated with starting both a production and distribution company that specialized in films depicting a strong Christian message in a town that had little use for such a message.

Through it all, none of us gave up. We believed that if we could weather the storm and just wait it out, things would eventually turn around for us. Little by little, year after year, we continued to make incremental progress. By the end of 2012, Pure Flix had managed to produce over fifteen films and distribute another fifty worldwide. The company had huge overhead, so none of us was getting rich, but that wasn't the goal. We were offering a positive and life-affirming message on an ongoing basis. It appeared as though our many years of waiting were paying off.

I found a quote while doing research for this book that sums it up pretty well. It's from Josiah Gilbert Holland, a nineteenth-century American novelist, who wrote, "There is no royal road to anything. One thing at a time, all things in succession. That which grows fast, withers as rapidly. That which grows slowly, endures."

Jesus's brother had these words for those who are called to wait: "Be patient, then, brothers and sisters, until the Lord's coming. See how the farmer waits for the land to yield its valuable crop, patiently waiting for the autumn and spring rains. You too, be patient and stand firm, because the Lord's coming is near" (James 5:7–8).

Farmers have it figured out, don't they? The farmer sows his seed in the properly plowed field. He doesn't see the grains immediately, but he waits for the rain and the sun to shine; he waits for the seeds to sprout and the shoots to grow. After months of work and waiting, he is rewarded with a harvest. James says we are to do the same: wait patiently for results.

It's much the same for you and your God-given dream. You've built the baseball diamond in your cornfield for underprivileged children, but will they come? You've established yourself as a tutor for homeschool students, but the telephone has yet to ring. Will you get a chance to improve the academic lives of grade school kids? I say if it's truly a God-given dream you've put into action, then you will, but you might have to wait longer for the harvest of your efforts than you expected.

GOD OF WAITING

Scripture is filled with examples that support the notion that God is a God of waiting. The Creator of the Universe takes his time to accomplish things. While he spent only six days on creating the universe, he has since then slowed down considerably, whether it's in answering our prayers, effecting a change in our lives, or implementing a major cultural shift. Most of the time, God isn't in any rush.

The book of James tells us to practice patience and perseverance through times of trial (James 1:4; 5:7–11). This isn't a very popular message for modern times. While I do not doubt the perfect theology or the divine inspiration of the book, I would like to humbly point out that it was written a couple of thousand years before the invention of the microwave oven. Or any other innovation of the last two hundred years that has contributed to the present fast-food, fast-track, fast-paced world we now live in. We evaluate the usefulness of any new invention based in part on how quickly it can do what it's supposed to do or how effectively it can eliminate our having to wait. Whether it's airplanes or computer processors, faster is better. Our tolerance for waiting seems to diminish with each passing decade. And when our fast-paced and hurried lifestyle, designed to "have it ready yesterday," collides with God's patient process, we find ourselves consumed with frustration, resentment, and sometimes anger.

If I had to guess, I'd say God is sometimes slow to move because he is eternal and therefore literally has all the time in the world. We as mortals, however, have a built-in deadline. Also, have you noticed how, as we get older, time moves so much faster? This phenomenon is a constant reminder of how little time we may have left. The phrase "Time is short" doesn't seem to mean much until you're older and you fear it's too late to do the things you want to do. We spend the second half of our life racing against the clock, trying to make plans to save time wherever we can.

As the Bible tells us: "In their hearts humans plan their course, but the LORD establishes their steps" (Proverbs 16:9). We all try to plan our lives, and when we were too young to do so, our parents and teachers did it for us. Most plans come with a timetable, or they're really not much of a plan. You have a timeline for going to college and starting a career. Your parents want you potty trained by a certain age, and your teachers hope to get you reading and writing by the third grade. It all makes sense.

The problem with schedules, timetables, and deadlines, however, is that they give us a false sense of who is in control. You might very well accomplish some of the things on your list by a certain deadline if you work hard enough and if it's God's will. As followers of Jesus, however, we must remain open to change. God may take you out of your fast lane and put you on another timetable.

WAITING ON GOD

I don't blame you if you've wondered if God sees, cares, or remembers you during your time of waiting. I spent eight years doing much the same thing. You tell yourself it's impossible that God would forget you, but sometimes it feels as though he has, making it even more difficult to wait for movement toward the fulfillment of your dream.

People have often asked me the value of Bible study, church, or fellowship. It was from studying God's Word on my own and from listening to solid biblical teaching at my church that

I learned to embrace the notion of waiting on God, his timing, and his direction for my life.

Here are a couple of passages that encouraged me most during the long period of waiting: "Since ancient times no one has heard, no ear has perceived, no eye has seen any God besides you, who acts on behalf of those who wait for him" (Isaiah 64:4). Waiting is not so bad when we realize God is a mover and a shaker, working behind the scenes. The outcome to whatever situation we face may not present itself in accordance to our timetable, but at some point God will get the job done.

The other verses are: "Be still before the Lord and wait patiently for him; do not fret when people succeed in their ways, when they carry out their wicked schemes. Refrain from anger and turn from wrath; do not fret—it leads only to evil" (Psalm 37:7–8). I like the phrase, "Be still." Some translations use the word *rest*. Either way, to me that means to relax, stop fighting it, go with God's flow. And don't get angry or resentful, because nothing good will come out of it. Lastly, don't worry about what the "other guy" is doing, be it his successes or his failures.

When we accept this, we live with what is called "hopeful expectation," which is fancy talk for having a positive outlook. We wake up each morning with a skip in our step; our hopeful expectation encourages us to participate in life with a sense of purpose even if we are uncertain as to the Lord's specific plan for us.

My father preached that God is sovereign, meaning there is absolutely nothing outside of his influence and command. How can any of us doubt this? God created the entire universe from his Word and his truth (John 1:1). Even if you feel defenseless against the curveballs life throws at you, your life is never out of control to the extent that God is unable to direct you, redeem you, or use you for his glory. The world may make you suffer, but stay brave! God has defeated the world (John 16:33)! Just because you don't understand or recognize what he is doing doesn't mean God is not working faithfully to bring about the dream he planted in your heart. His will and purpose won't be denied.

THE VALUE OF WAITING

There is value in waiting, although it rarely seems that way at the time. But if you keep your schedule over the Lord's, you run the risk of missing out on what he has in store for you. Sometimes we're just not ready for the things we want when we want them, and I believe that God tries to protect us from ourselves.

I can't imagine what my life would be like today if the Lord had allowed me the desires I thought I wanted at nineteen. I might very well have ended up as a sad Hollywood statistic. God made me wait for something I wanted immediately, and once again, God was right. Hindsight reveals he delayed events in my life for my own good. Waiting reminds us of or teaches us some simple truths.

We Learn Faith through Waiting

I know it's easy to be discouraged, but waiting on God for dream fulfillment can teach us important lessons about faith and how not to give up on God. We need to maintain our faith in order to please God (Hebrews 11:6). Isaiah 40:31 tells us, "But those who hope in the LORD will renew their strength."

People envision waiting as passive, but it's really an opportunity to *do something*. I found myself actively clinging to the Lord, resting in him, and keeping my thoughts centered on him.

These were decisions that strengthened my faith and required a call to action on my part.

Uncomfortable situations yield an opportunity for us to work the faith muscle. I believe sometimes God tells us to "take a number" and have a seat in order to demonstrate and teach us that "faith is confidence in what we hope for and assurance about what we do not see" (Hebrews 11:1).

We Learn Perspective through Waiting

Nothing is going to happen unless God wants it to. When you realize you aren't in control of the timing in your life, you realize that you really have no control over any of it. When things aren't happening according to our plans regardless of how hard we're trying, waiting teaches us absolute dependence on God, because he is the only one who can make things happen. We learn not to depend on ourselves or on our friends and family but only on God. Only God can make it happen. The sooner you realize you are helpless and that you need God, the less you might have to wait.

Do you really think God is going to allow you to rush him? Why pray for God to speed things up? Actually, why pray for anything that is not the Lord's will? Here's what you ought to say: "If it is the Lord's will, we will live and do this or that" (James 4:15). Why worry about things you have no control over? Hand over the control(s), and put God in the driver's seat.

We Learn Patience through Waiting

We have all heard that patience or forbearance is a virtue, and Paul tells us in his letter to the Galatians that patience is a fruit of the Spirit (5:22). Learning patience is a necessary part of our walk with the Lord and begins a process of spiritual maturity. If we choose to be patient while we wait on the Lord to fulfill our dream, we will naturally draw closer to him through prayer and worship. Patience is submission to his will, a demonstration that we are going to wait and rely on his timing.

THE DESIRES OF YOUR HEART

Many people believe, as I once did, that Psalm 37:4 is a guarantee that God is going to make our dreams come true. "Take delight in the Lord, and he will give you the desires of your heart." We want our desires and we want them now. But I think it's just as possible that God is saying that if we delight in him, then he will *instill* in us desires that he will delight in granting.

I remember that eight-year period in my life when Andrea and I were so desperate to get Pure Flix off the ground so we could make a living. I wasn't waiting to be rich; I just wanted to be able to pay the bills on time, and I did so by taking odd jobs like coaching acting on the Internet. But looking back, I realize I was still preoccupied with what our company's success should look like and when and how I believed it should happen. I was comparing Pure Flix to other companies and struggling to understand why they seemed to be doing okay, but we were still just keeping our heads above water.

As I said earlier, God's dream for us is really not about us. It's more about what he wants for us and what he wants to accomplish through us. It's about the desires he has placed in our hearts that he will delight in. We become God's messengers, delivering his will and his Word. Those years of waiting serve as a reminder of that truth. The years humbled me, changed my perspective, and I traded in my desires for his.

The waiting process can convert and transform you. I think God is more interested in the person we become while waiting on him than in the thing we're waiting on. I do the same with my own children. At times my son will ask me for a certain toy and I will tell him he has to wait for his birthday or for Christmas. I then pay special attention to how he behaves while he waits. Is he impatient, ungrateful, or demanding? Is it more important to him that he gets what he wants when he wants it than it is for him to trust in me that I know best? If he throws a tantrum, then he's just lost that GI Joe doll with the Kung Fu grip; but if he's accepting and patient, then I'm off to the store. Of course I want to make my son happy, but it's just as important to me that I see him mature in the process. I want to see graciousness, acceptance, and patience from my son before I grant his desires. God wants no less for his children.

Waiting can be torturous at any age. So how can you make this process bearable?

SURRENDER TO THE WAIT

Invite God into your plan. By taking your dreams and goals to the Lord, you demonstrate your acceptance of his will. Don't look at it like "if you can't beat 'em—join 'em." It's more like "I want to live the life God wants me to live because it's the best life for me to live." It's just a smart way to live your life, actually.

Trust that God knows what he's doing and that there are larger considerations in play. Sometimes your life isn't only about *your* life. Never underestimate the fact that there are others watching you and being influenced by your actions and faith. Your children, your spouse, or your friends and neighbors might one day be willing to place their trust in God as a result of your testimony of waiting. Don't make the mistake that you have to be a big star or be in the public eye in order to influence people. Your life is like a written testimony to all you meet.

To check out behind-the-scenes footage of David's film career as an actor, director, and producer, including never-before-seen photos on the set of God's Not Dead, *go to DavidARWhite.com/Exclusive.*

CHAPTER 9

If It Means Something to You, Give It Away

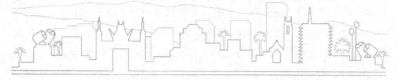

The purpose of life is to discover your gift. The work of life is to develop it. The meaning of life is to give your gift away.

David Viscott

By 2012, Pure Flix had released close to a hundred titles into the DVD market, which was our stated goal. We set out to provide faith-based content on a continual basis and to offer ongoing viewing options to the public. To do that, we had to put out a tremendous amount of product. To this end, we had made the decision to service the DVD market in Christian bookstores and other retailers worldwide.

The buyers—that is to say, the retail outlets like Family Christian, LifeWay, and Walmart—all loved us because we had become a trusted brand, and they could sell any of our products to a discerning customer without fear of reprisal or repercussion. Just as customers know what to expect when they watch a movie from Disney, our audience was learning that if a DVD said Pure Flix on the cover, then the content would be faith-based.

By this time, Andrea and I had three children, Ethan, Ocean, and Everson. As my family grew, I was thinking of ways for my company to grow as well.

For the past decade, Stephen and Alex Kendrick, leading members in my industry, have released an amazing movie for theatrical distribution every three years or so. The brothers' record is incredible. They did *Flywheel, Courageous, Fireproof,* and *Facing the Giants,* all to increasingly greater success. Until this point, my partners and I felt the Lord had led Pure Flix to go a slightly different way than the Kendrick brothers. We instead focused on providing content on an ongoing basis, not necessarily one big movie once every three years.

But at the end of 2012, we saw signs that the DVD market had started to soften because more and more people were buying subscriptions that allowed them to stream movies. This change caused us to rethink our strategy, and we started looking at ideas and screenplays for a wide theatrical release. We had already tested the market and our system in limited theatrical release with a couple of movies, including *What If,* but this time we had our eye on a nationwide release of over five hundred movie theater screens or more.

GOD'S NOT DEAD

Pure Flix hired Cary Solomon and Chuck Konzelman to write the screenplay for *God's Not Dead,* based loosely on the book *God's Not Dead: Evidence for God in an Age of Uncertainty* by Rice Broocks. The movie follows the character of Josh Wheaton, a Christian college student, whose faith is challenged by his college professor who announces at the beginning of the term that God is a prescientific fiction. Once the screenplay was complete, we had long conversations about which actors should play the leads.

Unlike the Kendrick brothers, who typically cast unknown actors in their movies, we thought that since we were going wide with the distribution, we wanted to consider name-brand actors with box-office drawing power. We considered a variety of actors to play the atheist Professor Radisson role, including Cuba Gooding Jr., for example, but in the end we decided to go with a good friend of ours, Kevin Sorbo, a fine actor we had worked with a few times before.

We auditioned quite a lot of folks for the Josh Wheaton role. Shane Harper didn't have the longest résumé, but he loved apologetics and the Lord and had a quality in his performance we thought drove the message of the movie home.

After we had decided on our cast, we chose Harold Cronk to direct. We had previously worked with Harold on a few movies, including *Jerusalem Countdown*, and we were confident he could deliver this movie as well.

I cast myself to play the role of Reverend Dave. I can't tell you how many times I've played a preacher of some kind in a movie. I guess I just have a preacher's face. Either that or I take after my dad.

God's Not Dead was shot in Baton Rouge, Louisiana. My first scene was filmed in October with Kevin Sorbo.

It was a very cold night, and the scene was to take place in the rain after Kevin Sorbo's character is struck by a car. As soon as I arrived on set, I was informed the writers had overwritten my scene with Kevin and most of the lines had to be cut. That kind of thing happens all the time in movie making, and it's not a big deal unless the actor has spent all week memorizing the lines. Actually this change turned out to be in my favor, because the heated water we had ordered for the rain did not show up and both of us had to perform this very tender and emotional salvation scene while gallons of freezing water poured down onto us. Somewhere during the third take, I began wishing the writers had cut the whole scene!

Once the movie was finished and "in the can," as they say in the film industry (although with a digital film there is no film can!), we faced the task of raising the money to market and distribute the film. This cost is generally referred to as P&A, or prints and advertising. Just to give you an idea of how expensive this can be, the average cost of P&A for a medium-sized film from a major studio release is over $40 million.

However, we weren't a major studio and had never taken a movie this wide before, so we were having difficulty raising the $5 million P&A funds we needed to release *God's Not Dead*. We shopped the film to several different studios, and they all turned us down. In the end, we were able to raise the money on our own and we distributed the film.

This was due in part to some amazing grassroots marketing. For instance, when we launched the trailer on Facebook, it was shared around ten million times during its first week, and it became the number one shared Facebook page in the world for that time.

We decided to feature a cameo appearance of Willie and Korie Robertson from the hugely popular reality TV show *Duck Dynasty*. It was a last-minute addition we thought our audience would enjoy. However, in December of that year, fellow cast member and patriarch of the Robertson clan Phil Robertson became the center of a controversy for some statements he made in *GQ* magazine. When A&E pulled Phil off their show, Christians came together to defend his position, and our hits on the websites continued to climb higher than anyone would have thought.

HOW WAS YOUR WEEKEND?

God's Not Dead was released theatrically on Friday, March 21, 2014. By the end of the weekend, we were the fourth highest-grossing movie in the country, preceded only by *Divergent*, *Muppets Most Wanted*, and *Mr. Peabody and Sherman*, all of which were in over 3,000 theaters while *God's Not Dead* premiered in only 780. Our little movie stayed in theaters for twenty weeks, became the number one live action independent film of the year, and according to the movie business website The Numbers, is still the sixth most profitable film, based on return on investment (ROI), in cinema history, ahead of the original *Star Wars* movie, *Jaws*, *Beauty and the Beast*, and even the classic *It's a Wonderful Life*.

So, yeah, that happened.

Variety, *Entertainment Tonight*, and many of the largest high-powered Hollywood agencies in the world wanted to know the secret of our success. I was asked about that over and over again. I guess the secret is, there is no secret. Not really. I've already shared with you how I got to where I am today. God put a dream in my heart to tell stories and make movies that glorified his name. As soon as I figured that out, that is what I did, and it is what I continue to do today. One of those movies happened to make a lot of money. That's pretty cool, I guess, but it didn't change anything for me or for my partners at Pure Flix.

I was asked by dozens of reporters what I planned to do now that I had the freedom to do what I *really* wanted to do. My answer was always the same: "I'm going to keep doing what I've been doing for the last fourteen years. I'm going to continue to make movies that spread the gospel."

You see, I'm not in the movie business for the fame or the fortune. I'm in it so that people's lives may be changed. Remember that scene I told you about with Kevin Sorbo, when gallons of freezing water were being dumped on our heads on a cold October night? That little scene, that one moment in the movie, touched so many people's lives. I have received so many emails from people telling me that it was a very impactful moment in their lives and some were brought to the Lord because of it. How much money is that worth? How many awards does that win? You can't begin to put a price tag on it. There is no trophy case big enough to house that kind of an award. Imagine that! Somebody receiving salvation through Jesus's grace because of a movie I made.

So, yeah, that happened too.

I came to Hollywood at the age of nineteen with the dream of working in the entertainment industry. I was not able to fulfill or realize that dream until I dedicated the dream to the service of others.

God placed the desire in my heart. He gave me the motivation to work on my craft. He gave me the talent and presented me with opportunities to fine-tune my craft. Over the years, I experienced several wins and losses, some ups and downs, and while I was often frustrated with the Lord's process, I realize now

I was meant to learn from it. My first decade or so in Hollywood prepared me for the moment when I would lay my dream down at the feet of the Lord and pledge to do it his way.

As I write this, I cannot help but hear my father's words the night I told him I wanted to go to Hollywood to pursue a career in acting. He told me, "As long as you serve the Lord, David, in whatever you do, your mom and I support you." It might as well have been God speaking. "As long as you serve me in whatever you do, I support you." One of the ways in which we serve God is by serving others. In Hebrews 13:16 we read, "And do not forget to do good and to share with others, for with such sacrifices God is pleased."

Albert Einstein is quoted as saying, "Only a life lived for others is the life worthwhile." I don't understand a lot of what Einstein wrote about, but that much I get.

The greatest servant of all was of course Jesus Christ, and he said, "The Son of Man did not come to be served, but to serve, and to give his life as a ransom for many" (Matthew 20:28).

EXPRESSING THE LOVE OF CHRIST THROUGH SERVICE

Most parents want to teach their children the value and virtue of sharing. As a father of three, I can tell you this is not always an easy task. It begins with motivating our kids to share toys and valued possessions, but later we learn the most valuable training resource we have is ourselves and how we use our time, our energy, and our talents for the purpose of serving others in the body of Christ.

Our best example for what it means to serve others is Jesus Christ. Paul said that Jesus took "the very nature of a servant" (Philippians 2:7). In John 13, we see an example of Christ's servitude when he washed the feet of his disciples. Much has been written about this amazing act of service, and I can do little here other than to share this anecdote from a movie I produced with Pure Flix.

When we were still conceptualizing the movie *Marriage Retreat*, one of our writers suggested that the best way, if not the most romantic, for the lead character Craig Sullivan to show his love and devotion to his wife was to have Sullivan, as played by actor Jeff Fahey, wash his wife's feet in a tender nightly ritual. The notion was that Sullivan led by serving his family and his wife. Sullivan washed his wife's feet, not in spite of the fact that he was the leader of his family, but *because* of it.

Few people, including myself, move to Hollywood in pursuit of a life dedicated to the service of others. Instead, most people strive to win at the Hollywood game so they can *be* served. We want to be the greatest in our field, whatever that field is, and reap the rewards and benefits. It's the American dream, right?

Jesus doesn't see the concept of greatness like most of the world does. In fact, his vision is so contrary to what we've been exposed to that sometimes even Christians have a hard time getting their heads around it. Even those who hung out with Jesus found themselves not getting it. The disciples argued over who was greater than the other (Mark 9:33–35). The mother of John and James went to Jesus and asked if her sons could have seats of high position next to Jesus in the afterlife (Matthew 20:20–22). We read these passages and we shake our heads, but are we really any different? We jockey and struggle for position and rank. We vie to keep up with the Joneses or to outdo them. We marshal all we have at our disposal, every last ounce of time and money, in order to claw our way to the top. This is what we have been taught. This is what we have been told.

The fact remains that if your dream is self-focused and self-centered, it will not come to pass. God requires that if you want something, you must first give it away. God demands that dreamers be generous with their talents, time, and love in order for the dream to come true. We must be humble and put the needs of others above our own selves.

I serve the Lord by serving others with the movies I make and distribute. I was charged with delivering the Word and promoting a culture for Christ through cinematic narrative, and I've taken some flak for it. A few of my films have been criticized for being heavy-handed, ham-fisted, and overly proselytizing. Frankly, some of the reviews from film critics are more imbued with hate and anger than with a sincere desire to criticize the artistic merits of the work. And I'm okay with that.

If your calling is to serve others by spreading the gospel, then remember one of the most generous things we can do is risk being mocked, hated, and reviled for spreading the Word of Christ. You always run the risk of having your God-given dream thrown back into your face, but don't let this stop you from sharing it. The gift I'm speaking of, that of grace and eternal life, is worth your taking it on the chin from time to time.

THE TIME IS NOW

Don't think that you have to achieve great things in your life before you can serve others. Don't wait for the time when you've already made it and now you can "give back." Wherever you are in your walk with the Lord, or whatever milepost you come upon along the road to dream fulfillment, know that the time to serve another is now. Don't put it off, for doing so stalls your own journey.

This is not a "someday" kind of thing I'm talking about. If you want to achieve your dreams, then generosity of the spirit is not an option. Unless you are willing to serve others, you limit what God is able to do through you and in you. Remember, your dream is not a vehicle for self-aggrandizement but rather an opportunity for God to work through you. You must embark to create this generous spirit now—right now. Procrastinate, make excuses, and put it off at your own peril.

Perhaps you're thinking, *What can I do to make a difference in someone's life?* Sadly, I hear this all too often. Please know that you don't need a special talent to serve others. It's not necessary that you be an artist or world-class athlete. God does not demand superhuman powers from us before he expects us to help others. If so, he would have a very short list of candidates to choose from. It takes no unique characteristics to help people, but it does take character.

Likewise, serving others doesn't require an unlimited bank account or connections to the White House. You can do simple things to serve others. Jesus washed feet. Paul built a fire on the island of Malta to warm his fellow shipwrecked passengers. You could stack chairs at the end of a church service or volunteer to babysit for the single mom next door. Each of these acts is simple and ordinary, but they highlight the giver's generous spirit, the ability to recognize a need, and then the commitment to answering that need.

Winston Churchill famously said, "What is the use of living, if it be not to strive for noble causes and to make this muddled world a better place for those who will live in it after we are gone?" All of us are surrounded by countless simple opportunities to show the love of God through caring actions toward others:

- On trash day, wheel an elderly neighbor's can out to the curb.
- Ask the grocery clerk to apply your unused coupons to another customer's items.
- Bake bread or cookies and deliver the food to a nearby fire station or group home.
- Shower the pediatric wing of a hospital with coloring books and crayons.

If you have a dream, live that dream now. Act and behave as though your dream has been fulfilled. Show the world and yourself what it would be like after you've achieved your dream. Cary Grant once said, "I pretended to be somebody I wanted to be until finally I became that person."

Here's a case in point. One stormy night many years ago, a couple in their midforties stumbled into a small Philadelphia hotel in search of a room to get out of the rain. The hotel manager, a friendly man with a winning smile, looked at the couple and explained that there were three conventions in town. "All of our rooms are taken," the manager said. "But I can't send a nice couple like you out in the rain at one o'clock in the morning. Would you perhaps be willing to sleep in my room? It's not exactly a suite, but it will be good enough to make you folks comfortable for the night." The husband and wife were of course extremely grateful. "God bless you," the wife reportedly said.

The next morning at the breakfast table, the couple sent the waiter to tell the manager they wanted to see him on important business. The manager went in, recognized the two people, sat down at the table, and said he hoped they had had a good night's sleep. They thanked him most sincerely. Then the husband astounded the clerk with this statement: "You're too fine a hotel man to stay in a hotel like this. How would you like for me to build a big, beautiful, luxurious hotel in the city of New York and make you general manager?"

The manager didn't know what to say. He thought there might be something wrong with their minds. He finally stammered, "It sounds wonderful." His guest then introduced himself. "I'm John Jacob Astor." The hotel he built would be known as the Waldorf Astoria and that manager, George Boldt, would indeed run it.

I don't tell you this story to entice you into thinking you will be rewarded for doing good deeds. The point here is that sometimes the most ordinary and mundane deeds can produce larger results than we expect. Simple acts can show the love of God through our actions.

ALL THAT GLITTERS

Hollywood was a strange place for me to learn the importance of serving others and how that service and my path to dream fulfillment were *inexorably woven together*. Most of the world has it backwards, but Hollywood especially defines success and greatness in terms of the four P's: power, possessions, prestige, and position. If you can snap your fingers and demand service from others; get a table in an overbooked, popular restaurant; or cut the line at a trendy nightspot, then you've made it, baby.

Regardless of what town we live in or what kind of work we may do, most of us live in a self-serving culture with a me-first mentality. Serving others is not a popular concept, and yet it's crucial in achieving your God-given dream. Remember, God put that dream in your heart for service, not self-interest. If you lack a servant's heart, then it will be all too easy to misuse your dream for personal glorification or gain. Welcome the prospect that your dream exists in order to meet the needs of others. While Jesus's apostles bickered over being able to sit in the seat closest to him, Jesus reminded them that greatness is measured in terms of service, not status.

Your dream is your ministry. The thing that burns in your heart and keeps you up at night is God's calling on you. I dreamed of being an actor and producing motion pictures. It took me years to realize it, but God was calling me to make movies in his name to glorify him. He wanted my work to witness to others, and only when I accepted this and was convicted to do it did I get to live my dream.

God wasn't interested in awards, accolades, or having my star on the Hollywood Walk of Fame. It was never about upscale dressing rooms, adoring fans, private jets, or limousines. God didn't care if I made a million dollars, and now I don't either. I want my body of work to impact our culture for Christ. God put the desire to make movies into my heart so that I could make a difference in his name. The movies I make serve both God and the audiences that enjoy them. The movies I make are acts of service that contain positive messages and share the gospel of Jesus Christ.

Through God, I live my dream.

To get an inside peek at the White's family photos, behind-the-scenes photos of the God's Not Dead *premiere, and some of David's favorite films,* Revelation Roads, Brother White, The Encounters, *and more, visit DavidARWhite.com/Exclusive.*

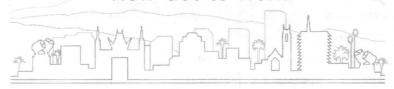

CHAPTER 10

Now Get to Work

*Turn my heart toward your statutes and
not toward selfish gain. Turn my eyes
away from worthless things; preserve
my life according to your word.*

Psalm 119:36–37

A short time after *God's Not Dead* came out and made a lot of noise at the box office, Alex Kendrick called both to congratulate and warn me. He told me to watch out, stay vigilant, and prepare myself to be soon hit with a lot of tribulation and temptation. He said that success puts a big bull's-eye on your back. You become a target for Satan when you begin to live your God-given dream because, frankly, you've ticked him off. To ward off his rage, you must stay centered and balanced through a close relationship with Jesus Christ. Jesus is our last line of defense against he who would delight in our failure.

In this chapter I want to leave you with a warning as well.

Maybe you've followed some of the principles in this book and were able to live your God-given dream. Perhaps reading this book has helped you discover that you are already living your dream, but you didn't recognize it. If you have discovered God's dream for you and have begun to live it, I'm very happy for you. It's a wonderful and glorious thing to be walking in the steps God forged for you at the dawn of time. But life during the dream-living phase doesn't come without its challenges. It's important to keep grounded and focused.

In this chapter I'd like to share with you some simple principles that have been helpful to me.

AVOID THE BUSY TRAP

Have you heard the news? Being "busy" is no longer respectable. Neither is being too busy a suitable excuse for ignoring the important aspects of life like the Word of God, your health, and those closest to you. Screenwriter and novelist Nigel Marsh said, "Often, people work long hard hours at jobs they hate to earn money to buy things they don't need, to impress people they don't like."

Busyness is often a form of self-aggrandizement that can lead to an addiction of sorts. Busy people are important, right? They believe nothing will get done and the world will stop spinning on its axis without their tireless and relentless input. Ironically, recent studies illustrate that those who continually stay busy are often unproductive, and extreme busyness can be a symptom of a person's inability to properly manage their life.

Of course there are always going to be periods when we are legitimately busier than others. Everyone knows the crunch of deadlines, adjusting to a new baby, buying or selling a home, or dealing with an illness. I'm talking more about those folks who for their own reasons are *always* busy. It's more than likely a sign they are not living within their means, or that they lack the ability to prioritize efficiently, or that they have a problem saying no to further and mounting responsibility.

Do you feel the twenty-four hours offered in a day are simply not enough to complete the tasks on your plate? If so, you might be falling into the busyness trap.

Our culture promotes the idea that bigger, newer, and faster is better, and it can be tempting to feel you must keep up. The Bible warns us not to allow ourselves to be swept away by our society's undercurrent. Romans 12:2 says, "Do not conform to the pattern of this world, but be transformed by the renewing of your mind. Then you will be able to test and approve what God's will is—his good, pleasing and perfect will."

If you're living your dream, odds are you're going to be busy, and it's probably going to feel great. You may say you feel more alive, that your life has never had such purpose, and it can be intoxicating. Be careful, however, because this sensation cannot be sustained in the long term. Ultimately, be it today or tomorrow or in those moments before you meet your Maker, you're going to wish that you had spent fewer hours living to work versus working to live. Busyness for busyness's sake is a trap, a limbo where the act of "staying busy" masks fruitless results and the inability to achieve goals.

I used to feel I had to do it all, but I've learned that giving up a little control has cleared my plate. These days, instead of micromanaging people, I try to delegate tasks and responsibilities to others, which eases my daily burden. In addition I try to not take on more than I know I can handle. If an opportunity or task presents itself that I feel is beyond my reach, I either delay or postpone it to a point when I know I'll have more time. Either that, or I simply say no.

UNPLUG

The Bible encourages us to occasionally get away from it all so that we may recharge our spiritual batteries and spend some alone time with God. Even Jesus understood the value of rest and a peaceful atmosphere and would occasionally withdraw from the crowds to renew his strength. "Then, because so many people were coming and going that they did not even have a chance to eat, he said to them, 'Come with me by yourselves to a quiet place and get some rest'" (Mark 6:31). Sometimes God speaks in a quiet voice, and we run the risk of missing it if we're too absorbed in the rat race of our twenty-first-century world.

Here are some tips that I find particularly useful:

- Turn off the computer. Really, it's okay. The social network can get by without you for the day. Likewise, you'll do just fine having not watched those last five cat videos. The computer may allow you to connect to the world at large, but don't allow it to disconnect you from your family and loved ones.
- Go to bed earlier and get more sleep. Too many of us don't get enough sleep, but lack of sleep is associated with a surprisingly long laundry list of serious problems, including an increased risk of obesity, diabetes, stroke, and an earlier death.
- Turn off your cell phone. Your cell phone is probably exposing you to more radiation than anyone would care to think about, but that's not the whole problem. People have become attached to their cell phones to such an extent that when they're taken away for even short

periods of time, they go through separation anxiety. This is a sign we've become too dependent on them, and they're interfering with our lives.

- Unplug the television. Stow the video game console. Turn off the stereo. You hear that? It's called quiet. Enjoy it. You would be amazed what you can hear in the quiet.

KEEP YOUR COMPASS SET TO TRUE NORTH

Everyone knows what a compass is and what it is used for. It's a little gizmo that always points north in order to orient you so you don't get lost. Did you know, however, that a compass can become unreliable from magnetic force field interference? Sailors, for instance, are aware the compass needs to be positioned in such a manner that it is shielded from potential interference, ensuring the compass readings are always true.

Shield Yourself

Hollywood and the motion picture business provide for a lot of "interference" that can gum up the works of my internal moral compass. However, it matters little what town you live in or what field you work in, because there are forces at war against righteousness everywhere you go.

Ancient Jews were aware of these course-altering influences and how vulnerable people were to them as soon as they left their homes. They therefore were required by law to tack Scriptures on their doorposts (Deuteronomy 6:9). The Scriptures called out to them when they left home and questioned them when they returned. These Scriptures, typically housed in a decorative case called a mezuzah, shielded believers as they went about their days.

While I haven't hung a mezuzah from my doorpost, I do value Scripture and recognize its protective qualities. When I was a kid, my father used to pay me ten cents for every note I would take during one of his sermons. He knew how easy it is for people's minds to wander during the sermon, and he wanted to motivate me to pay attention. It's easy to tune out on a Sunday morning when we're thinking about how hungry we are or how our favorite football team is going to perform that day. Taking notes in the sermon caused me to stay focused. At first I did it for the money, but as I grew older I began to appreciate the practice for its own merit, and eventually it became a habit.

Today I post my sermon notes on my Facebook page. Not only does this help me to focus in church, but it also allows me to share the notes with all of my Facebook friends. In doing this I am building a cloak of protection around myself. I always appreciate it when my Facebook friends post back their own notes. It's encouraging and supportive. It's a way of putting Hebrews 10:24–25 into practice: "And let us consider how we may spur one another on toward love and good deeds, not giving up meeting together, as some are in the habit of doing, but encouraging one another—and all the more as you see the Day approaching."

I've also found help for keeping my compass set to true north by using the Bible as my moral compass—by allowing it to define who I am.

Make God's Word Your Moral Compass

When I first moved to Hollywood, I soon discovered how lost I was without my *Thomas Guide*, a detailed map of Los Angeles County. Then I relied heavily on MapQuest, and now I can't seem to find my way out of my driveway without a GPS. We all need maps or specific directions to navigate the highways and byways of life. Without them we can become lost, and this is never a good thing.

Likewise, we need a moral compass to navigate through life. A moral compass without the principles of God's Word is useless and ineffective. There are many Sundays when the last thing I want to do is get up and haul the kids to church, but we all need to know God's Word and what it says about how we are to live. And if you're living your dream, then you might be particularly in need of some humility and direction.

Of course our popular culture sends a very different message, especially out here in Tinseltown. We are immersed in a culture of moral relativism that says we can make up the rules as we go along and that we should not judge other people's behavior.

As our country moves toward the notion of universal acceptance, I believe we are at the same time building our houses in the sand. The parable of the wise and foolish builders illustrates what happens when we try to set up shop on a weak foundation. "But everyone who hears these words of mine and does not put them into practice is like a foolish man who built his house on sand. The rain came down, the streams rose, and the winds blew and beat against that house, and it fell with a great crash" (Matthew 7:26–27).

It might be tempting to live a life without rules, especially for young people, but what happens when you turn your back on God's instruction? You have no baseline to make decisions. How much is too much? How far is too far? God has already worked these things out for you, so why challenge him? Even just a short time away from the Lord can lead to a lifetime of remorse.

Reset Yourself

I start every day on my knees in prayer. It's a humbling way to kick off the day and a reminder that I live to serve God. This act of humility gives me courage and strength. I found a quote on the Internet, and although its author is anonymous, I think it sums it up: "When you start your day on your knees, you are able to stand for or against anything the day brings."

The noise and clamor of the day can distract me, and I can find myself obsessing over the trivial and unimportant. Sometimes it's good to take a break and reevaluate where you're headed and what you did to get to where you are. Sometimes I will just put on the brakes for a moment to ground myself in prayer. In this way I can discover a sense of renewal and direction that will ultimately keep me on course. Your moral compass may need to be reset occasionally. Are you doing too much of what you want simply because you can get away with it? Are you ignoring the consequences of your actions? Are you trying to strategize and conceive of ways to get around biblical guidelines? Are you trying to outthink the Word of God? Has your threshold for risky and questionable behavior grown with your ego and sense of self-importance?

If you answered yes to any of the above, then it may be time to realign your moral compass and get back to basics.

You're a Target Now

Alex Kendrick was right. If you're living your God-given dream, then you are in some way bringing to earth the influence of the kingdom of God as it is in heaven. How do you think that sits with Satan or any other who possesses an agenda that opposes what God wants to do on this earth? The devil will focus his attention on those who present the biggest threats to his ambitions. This is not the time to get spiritually lazy or to drop your guard. You will have to remain just as vigilant and prayerful as you were before you were living out the dream God placed in your heart.

Thank you for taking this journey with me. We started just outside of Dodge City, Kansas, and ended in Hollywood, California, and I think that's proof right there that dreams can come true. I never promised you it would be a journey easily completed and that there wouldn't be twists and detours along the way. I hope you remember that, generally speaking, nothing worth having comes easy.

As our journey nears its finish line, there is one final point I'd like to make.

You are worth it, and your dream is worthy of you. These two concepts are difficult for many to accept, but in the end, know this: God chose you to fulfill the dream he placed in your heart. He believes that you are the best candidate to see it through. So have faith in God. He surely has faith in you.

I hope the principles and experiences I've shared will help you in your journey to pursue your God-given dream. Trust God to guide you and to provide you with the courage to step out in faith. Today is your day to act. Don't put it off a second longer. Good luck, and God bless you!

To see on- and off-the-set photos of Faith of Our Fathers, Do You Believe, *and never-before-seen photos of David as Randy Wilcox in his new sitcom called* Hitting the Breaks, *go to DavidARWhite.com /Exclusive.*

Epilogue

As I said before, things are happening so fast for me and for Pure Flix that it was difficult to decide where and when in my journey to end this book. After I sent the first draft to the publishers, something remarkable happened that I felt strongly about including.

I recently just completed production on a sitcom called *Hitting the Breaks,* a sitcom where my wife and I star in a show about an ex-race-car driver who must abandon a lifelong dream in order to adopt a new one. My character, Randy Wilcox, inherits a bed-and-breakfast bequeathed by his departed father. After moving into the hotel, Randy discovers a series of never-mailed letters written to him by his dad. Each episode ends with Randy reading one of these letters, which are imbued with biblical wisdom and spiritually guided advice. The thought was, after I read a few lines of the letter, my voice would fade out and be replaced by the actor playing the role of Randy's father.

Several name-brand actors were suggested when it came time to cast the role of my father in the show, but I had my hopes on Burt Reynolds. I put the offer out to his agents and hoped for the best. I can't express the sense of irony I felt when he accepted. The man who gave me my start in his sitcom, my

Hollywood mentor and beloved on-set father figure, was about to reenter my life some two decades later, this time to perform in my sitcom.

I flew to Burt's hometown of Jupiter, Florida, to record his voice-overs, and during the trip over I read his newly published autobiography. I was startled to learn Burt was born in the same year as my father.

As I stepped into the tiny recording studio where I was to work with Burt, I wondered if he would remember me. I admit I was nervous. When Burt came into the studio, he greeted me warmly, and after a few moments I realized that after almost twenty-five years since I saw him last, he was still Burt Reynolds. Yes, he was older, as I was too, but the quality that made him Hollywood's top box-office draw for five years in a row was still there. I spent two days with Burt recording his part for my new sitcom, and when I left he hugged me, told me he was proud of me, and that he loved me. It reminded me very much of the last time I spoke to my father.

As I write this, I'm back on the plane returning to Los Angeles. I'm staring out the window reliving the last forty-eight hours, and I still can't believe what has unfolded. And I'm reflecting.

I spent so many of my early years in Hollywood wishing I could be like Burt Reynolds. Since I started living the dream that God put in my heart, I feel so very happy, grateful, and blessed that I turned out to be David A.R. White.

Acknowledgments

Thank you to my wonderful family I'm so blessed to have around! To my kids, Ethan, Ocean, and Everson: I love your hearts, minds, and sense of humor. To my wife, Andrea: Thanks so much for always being there for me. I love your heart, mind, and passion. Thanks for spending your life with me. Through it all, you are my babe!

I want to thank my business partners, Michael Scott, Elizabeth Travis, and the late Russell Wolfe. For so many years we started with nothing, and against all odds, we dreamed, worked, and achieved together. I'd also like to thank our entire Pure Flix team for their perseverance, commitment, and strength. And a big thanks to Mani Sandoval and his team at Sandoval Design & Marketing for all the help on my social media—you are truly my rock star!

I'm blessed to have had many friends over the years. I can't list all of you for lack of space; however, I'd like to thank my brothers who have been with me throughout almost all of my years in Hollywood: Brad Heller, Kevin Downes, Jon Gunn, and Jeff Peterson. We've had so many highs and lows, and you guys have been with me through it all. Thank you.

To my editor, Sandy Vander Zicht: Thank you for believing

in this book from the beginning. It wouldn't have happened without you and the rest of the amazing Zondervan team: David Morris, Alicia Kasen, and Bob Hudson.

I want to thank my friend Tommy Blaze, who has helped me write so many different things over the years—from scripts and web shows, to movies and stand-up, to this book. Thank you, Tommy Blaze—you're so fun to be around and to act with. I look forward to many more years and things to do together! I appreciate you, man!

I'd of course like to thank my agent, Shannon Litton, of 5by5. Shannon, you're my wife's and my agent, but more importantly, you and your husband, Joel, are our dear friends. Thanks for being there for us and believing in us. Mike Schatz, you are the man! Appreciate all you've been doing for me, and can't wait to work on a whole lot more stuff together!

To all my fans, I just want to say thank you for all your support. I love that you watch our films, and I am grateful for all the support over the years. This and everything I do, I dedicate to you all!